Politics and
Government in China

The *Understanding China Today* series offers students and general readers the opportunity to thoroughly examine and better understand the key contemporary issues that continue to keep China in the news and sometimes at the center of global controversy. These issues include business, technology, politics, government, civil liberties, family life, and gender concerns, among others.

Narrative chapters in each volume provide an introduction and brief history of the topic, followed by comprehensive discussions of the subject area as it pertains to China's present and future. With each volume, specialists and scholars present a solid, up-to-date foundation for learning about contemporary China, written in an accessible, engaging manner.

As the world moves into the second decade of the 21st century, China's position on the global stage is more prominent than ever. The *Understanding China Today* series provides vital insight into this international powerhouse for new generations of students, and others, seeking to understand a complex, ever-changing nation with a future as fascinating as its past.

Politics and Government in China

GUOLI LIU

Understanding China Today

ABC-CLIO

Santa Barbara, California • Denver, Colorado • Oxford, England

Library of Congress Cataloging-in-Publication Data

Liu, Guoli, 1961–
  Politics and government in China / Guoli Liu.
    p. cm. — (Understanding China today)
  Includes bibliographical references and index.
  ISBN 978–0–313–35730–5 (hard copy : alk. paper) — ISBN 978–0–313–35731–2
(ebook)
1. China—Politics and government—20th century. 2. China—Politics and government—
21st century. I. Title. II. Series: Understanding China today.
DS775.7.L57   2011
951.05—dc22   2011014146

ISBN: 978–0–313–35730–5
EISBN: 978–0–313–35731–2

15 14 13 12 11   1 2 3 4 5

This book is also available on the World Wide Web as an eBook.
Visit www.abc-clio.com for details.

ABC-CLIO, LLC
130 Cremona Drive, P.O. Box 1911
Santa Barbara, California 93116-1911

This book is printed on acid-free paper ∞

Manufactured in the United States of America

Contents

Acknowledgments

I would like to thank Kaitlin Ciarmiello, acquisitions editor at ABC-CLIO, for her strong support and valuable assistance. Kaitlin has fully participated from the planning stage to the editing process of the manuscript. She searched for the beautiful photos for the book.

My colleagues and students at the College of Charleston provide a great learning environment. I am grateful for their help in many ways.

List of Abbreviations

APC	Agricultural Producers' Cooperative
CCP	Chinese Communist Party
CCRG	Central Cultural Revolution Group
CCTV	China Central Television
CCYL	Chinese Communist Youth League
CMC	Central Military Commission
CMS	Cooperative Medical Scheme
CPPCC	Chinese People's Political Consultative Conference
FDI	Foreign Direct Investment
GDP	Gross Domestic Product
GLF	Great Leap Forward
KMT	Kuomintang (Chinese Nationalist Party)
NPC	National People's Congress
NPCSC	National People's Congress Standing Committee
PLA	People's Liberation Army
PPP	Purchasing Power Parity
PRC	People's Republic of China
SAR	Special Administrative Region

SARS   Severe Acute Respiratory Syndrome
SEZ   Special Economic Zone
SOE   State-Owned Enterprise
SPC   Supreme People's Court
SPP   Supreme People's Procuratorate
WTO   World Trade Organization

Introduction: Understanding Chinese Politics

Governing China, the most populous country in the world, has always been challenging. It is particularly challenging in the age of globalization. As its economy grows rapidly, China's cultural exchange and economic interaction with the outside world are expanding quickly. Chinese politics, however, remain a puzzle to many outsiders. This book examines the key issues in contemporary Chinese politics.

The introduction highlights some key themes for understanding Chinese politics. Chapter 1 provides a historical overview of the politics of the People's Republic of China (PRC). Chapter 2 focuses on China's leaders and leadership transition. Chapter 3 examines the evolution of the Chinese Communist Party from a revolutionary party to a governing party. Chapter 4 looks at state institutions and policy making. Chapter 5 focuses on economic development and social transition. Chapter 6 examines law and order. The final chapter will look at China's place in a changing world.

THE PUZZLES OF CHINESE POLITICS

What are the main puzzles in Chinese politics? What are the driving forces for change in Chinese politics? Why did China not develop

Western-style capitalism and democracy? Why have Chinese politics experienced so many dramatic and profound transitions in the last century? Why has China's polity been relatively stable since 1990 in spite of (or because of) rapid economic growth? Are Chinese politics lagging behind China's rapidly growing economy? Why has the Chinese Communist Party (CCP) survived, while the majority of the communist parties in Central and Eastern Europe collapsed? Is the official ideology of the CCP inconsistent with the demands of globalization? What are the connections between reform and opening? In other words, is reform driving China's opening up? Or is opening up driving China's domestic reforms? Will economic development and the rise of a middle class lead to democratization of the Chinese political system? What are the central contradictions in Chinese politics and society today?

The above questions are some of the puzzles of Chinese politics. Although there are no ready answers to most of the questions, this book aims to provide a foundation and framework for readers to explore such critical questions. It is reasonable to argue that the driving forces for change in Chinese politics come from inside and outside of the country. Inside China, the people demand a higher living standard and a life with more freedom and dignity. Externally, global competition is forcing China to make adjustments so it will not fall behind in the era of globalization. In its search for modernity, China has experienced major twists and turns because the country has faced unprecedented domestic and international challenges. Hundred of schools of thinking have competed to win the hearts and minds of Chinese intellectuals and other citizens. In their quest for modernization and national identity, some Chinese leaders have adopted a trial and error approach. That might explain why China has experimented with so many different types of political systems and policies.

After many decades of turbulent changes, there emerged a strong popular demand for stability in the early 1990s. The Chinese elites also reached a relatively high degree of consensus about the need for stability. Since 1990, Chinese politics have been relatively stable because of such popular demand and elite consensus. However, there are growing social tensions and policy differences. That is why the current leadership calls for social harmony and political stability. Whether such calls can be realized depends on the leadership's ability to bridge the gap between economic reform and political change.

More and more farsighted leaders and intellectuals have realized that without timely and profound political reform, China's economic transition might be trapped. Any serious political reform will involve redistribution of power and resources. There will be winners and losers. The CCP survived a legitimacy crisis while most other communist parties failed, because the CCP realized the need for reform sooner and carried out more effective economic reforms. Economic development has provided some popular support for the regime while the role of ideology has declined. The official ideology has lost its traditional appeal and has been subjected to reinterpretation. Numerous attempts have been made to adjust the ideology according to the changing times. So far the CCP has not been able to build a new ideology that fits well with the current era of marketization, democratization, and globalization.

When China began its reform and opening in 1978, the reform was clearly driving its opening policy. Opening to the outside world was a means to achieve the end of modernization. After its initial success and then the crisis of 1989, Deng Xiaoping and other reformers argued that the only way for China to move forward was to deepen reform and opening. As China continues to reform and further opens its door, especially after Chinese entry to the World Trade Organization in 2001, it appears clear that reform and opening are mutually strengthening. China cannot continue its reform without further opening up. The opening policy cannot succeed without deeper reform. In the following sections, we will examine change and continuity and some key challenges facing Chinese politics.

CHANGE AND CONTINUITY

What aspects form the change and continuity in Chinese politics? What are the constant themes and what are the new elements of Chinese politics? From 1910 to 2010, China went through the collapse of the last imperial dynasty, the creation of a republic, warlord politics, Japanese invasion, civil war, the establishment of the People's Republic of China, land reform, socialist transition, the Cultural Revolution, and reform and opening. It seems that change is constant. One set of policies was replaced by a new set and one group of leaders was replaced by another group, sometimes orderly and often unexpectedly.

Tiananmen (Gate of Heavenly Peace). (Photograph taken by Guoli Liu.)

Is tradition still alive? What belongs to the core of Chinese tradition? What is the relevance of Chinese traditional schools of thinking, including Confucianism, Daoism, or legalism? What about Sun Yat-sen's three principles of the people? Is the call for science and democracy that was championed by the May Fourth Movement still valid today? What is the essence of Mao Zedong's "New Democracy"? What are the core elements of Deng Xiaoping's theory? What is new about Jiang Zemin's "three represents"? What is unique about Hu Jintao's call for social harmony and a scientific development perspective?

What are the major changes? Modernization, urbanization, information revolution, and communication revolution are taking place simultaneously in China today. The most important changes include the following: China is moving from a traditional society to a modern society; from a planned economy to a market economy; from a rural society to an urban society; from the rule of person (*renzhi*) to an emerging rule of law; from an isolated country to a country with extensive ties to the outside world; from revolution to reform; from arbitrary leadership succession to institutionalized leadership transition; and from tightly controlled and limited information to still-managed but increasingly diverse channels of communication. The role of ideology has been clearly in decline. Change is the norm in China today. Changes are taking place everywhere.

In this era of rapid change, there are some elements of continuity in Chinese politics and society. In the modernization process, Confucianism has not disappeared. On the contrary, it is enjoying some degree of revival. Professor Yu Dan's lectures on Confucianism on China Central Television (CCTV) in 2006 and her book on *Analects* published in 2007 were enormously popular in China. In spite of all the political change, the CCP remains the ultimate power in Chinese politics. There are still no effective checks and balances at the top level. There is no direct election for key leadership positions in the party and the government. China remains a unitary state in which the center directly appoints all key officials in the provinces. The military remains under the direct control of the CCP. With all the progress in marketization, China's banking, electricity, telecommunication, railway, airline, and other key industries are still heavily regulated by the state. The state still has controlling shares in the most important industries. The state budgetary system remains highly centralized and quite secretive. Economic development remains the top priority of the party and the state as well as a key source of legitimacy.

FREE MARKET ECONOMY AND AUTHORITARIAN POLITICS

From the socialist transition in the1950s to 1978, China was building a planned economy. The market was considered a feature of capitalism and thus was systematically suppressed. It was very dangerous to even talk about the market. Since reform began in 1978, however, Chinese reformers have gradually realized that there is no alternative to the market in the search for building a dynamic modern economy. By 1993, the CCP officially announced its goal of building a market economy in China. There is no doubt that China is developing a market economy. Can the authoritarian political system continue to coexist with the market? Will the growing middle class demand more channels of communication and participation? How will the rise of the Internet and growing number of netizens affect Chinese politics?

"Market Leninism" has been used by Western scholars and journalists to describe the Chinese system. The phrase highlights the combination of a free market economy and authoritarian politics. As a result of the global financial crisis during 2008–2009 and Beijing's relatively effective response to the crisis, there are some scholars who suggest perhaps this "Chinese model" is more effective than the laissez-faire system advocated by economic liberals in the West. But it remains to be seen whether the Chinese system can adapt to the challenge of sustainable growth. Even if the system works relatively well in China, it may not be applicable to other countries. Beijing economist Yang Yao has seriously questioned the validity of the so-called Beijing consensus. Yao argues that the authoritarian growth is not sustainable. If China wishes to continue its high growth rate on a sustainable basis, it must make the transition to democracy and the rule of law.

Authoritarian politics might be useful in the initial stage of modernization, when the country needs to make many painful decisions, facing numerous conflicting demands. As the economy develops and the society becomes more pluralistic, however, authoritarian rule will face growing challenges from below. If the popular demands for more freedom are not met, the growing tensions between state and society might lead to severe social conflicts and political instability. It is reasonable to argue that China's market reform will promote more political liberalization over the long run. More political opening, in turn, can further allow the market to mature.

RAPID GROWTH AND GROWING DISPARITY

China has experienced more than three decades of rapid economic growth. Economic development has improved the lives of the majority of the Chinese people. More than 400 million people have escaped poverty in the era of reform and opening. Economic growth, however, has not resulted in the reduction of rural and urban divide. In reality, the rural and urban income gap has grown significantly in the last three decades.

There are winners and losers from the market reform and opening to the outside world. The household responsibility system implanted

Table 1. Household Consumption Expenditure in Yuan

Year	All Households	Rural Household	Urban Household	Urban/Rural Consumption Ratio (Rural Household = 1)
1978	184	138	405	2.9
1980	238	178	489	2.7
1985	446	349	765	2.2
1990	833	560	1596	2.9
1995	2355	1313	4931	3.8
2000	3632	1860	6850	3.7
2005	5463	2560	9410	3.7
2008	6183	3756	13526	3.6

Source: *China Statistical Yearbook 2009*, Beijing, 2009, p. 61.

during 1979–1980 significantly benefited the farmers. In the early reform, the majority of the people were winners. In the 1990s, as urban income grew faster, rural income lagged behind. As Table 1 indicates, in 1978, the rural and urban household expenditure gap was only 267 yuan. By 2008, the gap widened to 9770 yuan.

Income gaps and regional disparities have grown significantly in China. As beneficiaries of preferential government policies, the special economic zones along the southern Chinese coast and the open cities in the coastal area moved ahead of the rest of the country in growth rate. Deng Xiaoping actually encouraged some people and some regions to become rich first. In a large and diverse developing country, it is impossible to make the country grow evenly. The preferential policies have accelerated the pace of growth in the more developed areas and strengthened their comparative advantages. According to Table 2, the household expenditure gaps among Beijing (20346 yuan), Shanghai (27343), Guizhou (4426), and Tibet (3504) in 2008 were enormous. The nearly eight-times difference between Shanghai and Tibet is unfair and unsustainable. In recent years, the Chinese government has initiated an ambitious plan to develop the less-developed areas of China. It remains to be seen whether the "Western region development plan" can help to narrow the income gap between the prosperous Eastern coastal areas and the less-developed vast Western region.

Table 2. Household Consumption Expenditure by Selected Region in Yuan (2008)

Region	All Household	Rural Household	Urban Household	Urban/Rural Ratio (Rural Household = 1)
Beijing	20346	10043	22207	2.2
Shanghai	27343	12202	29250	2.4
Jiangsu	11013	6461	14930	2.3
Zhejiang	13893	7665	18515	2.4
Guangdong	14390	5176	19743	3.8
Guizhou	4426	2142	10106	4.7
Shaanxi	6290	2993	10965	3.7
Tibet	3504	2149	8324	3.9
Gansu	4869	2480	9975	4.0

Source: *China Statistical Yearbook 2009*, Beijing, 2009, p. 62.

There has been a growing trend of concentration of wealth into the hands of a small number of people. The housing prices in urban China have been rising much faster than household incomes. It is becoming increasingly difficult for people with average incomes to purchase their own homes. At the same time, the costs of health care and education have been growing faster than the growth of personal income. Popular discontent about the rising income gap is increasing quickly. That discontent is particularly acute if the well-to-do obtained their wealth by corruption and other illegal or extralegal means.

RULE BY VIRTUE OR RULE BY LAW

Confucianism emphasizes the rule of virtue (*de*), while modern society requires the rule of law. Without an effective system of checks and balances, the rule of virtue is not reliable. What if a good ruler turns bad? The result might be catastrophic without the effective checks of a well-functioning legal system. Mao Zedong's unchecked power caused the failures of the Great Leap Forward and the Cultural Revolution. The rule of one person is unpredictable and unreliable.

China's reformers from Deng Xiaoping to today's Hu Jintao have all talked about the importance of building the rule of law. Rule by law is different from the rule of law. In rule by law, law is considered an instrument for the rulers. In the rule of law, everyone, including the top officials, should be equal before the law. Law has the highest authority. In a system dominated by the CCP, however, law is often subjected to interference by politics. In today's China, "rule by law" might be closer to reality than the ideal rule of law. If an issue of criminal conduct involves a high-ranking official, for instance, the state criminal system will not be able to take decisive action until the CCP disciplinary committee first conducts its investigation and takes action against the official.

Some Chinese scholars believe that China can implement the rule of law without a democratic system. They point to the success of Singapore, Hong Kong, or even Japan as cases of the rule of law functioning without full democracy. Other scholars contend that the rule of law will not work without democracy. In the absence of a democratic system, it is impossible to establish effective checks and balances. When the highest officials are not elected by the people, it is difficult to hold them accountable to the public.

To achieve full modernity, China must move toward the rule of law. With 2,000 years of autocratic rule, however, it will take China a long time to firmly establish the rule of law.

CORRUPTION AND LEGITIMACY CRISIS

With the decline of traditional ideology and the rise of money worship, corruption has indeed become a life and death issue for the ruling CCP. There is no doubt that uncontrolled corruption will undermine the legitimacy of the CCP. Economic growth provides additional incentive and opportunity for official corruption to take place.

There are three major sources of legitimacy as described in Max Weber's conceptions of traditional, charismatic, and legal-rational authority. In China, traditional legitimacy is passing away, and charismatic authority is declining, if not totally disappearing. Legal-rational authority is emerging but not well established yet. Over the long run, legal-rational authority is the wave of the future. In a society with deep historical burden, however, it remains to be seen how long it will take China to establish legal-rational authority as its fundamental source of legitimacy.

There is a paradox in Chinese politics. Corruption is rampant because the rule of law is weak. Legitimacy is weak because of widespread corruption. Combating corruption requires a strong system based on the rule of law. Many Chinese reformers have recognized the pivotal role of the rule of law. A critical issue is how to make sure that the highest power can be effectively checked by the law. No individual or institution should be above the constitution. The full implementation of constitutionalism will be a true testimony of China's move toward modernity.

Chronology

1911   Revolution breaks out in many parts of China. Sun Yat-sen becomes provisional president of a republican government before it comes to national power.

1912   The last emperor of the Qing dynasty abdicates, and the Republic of China is established. Gen. Yuan Shikai takes control of the Republic. Sun Yat-sen founds the Kuomintang (Chinese Nationalist Party).

1915   Japan wants China as a protectorate in the "Twenty-One Demands." Yuan Shikai attempts to restore the monarchy and make himself emperor.

1916   Yuan Shikai dies. China is dominated by many warlords.

1919   The May Fourth Movement begins, with protest against the terms of the Versailles Treaty and against the weak leaders of China, ushering in a period of political and cultural ferment. The students also demand democracy and science.

1921   The Chinese Communist Party (CCP) is founded with assistance from the Moscow-based Comintern.

1923   The First United Front between the CCP and the Kuomintang (KMT) against the warlords is formed.

1925   Sun Yat-sen dies.

1926   The Northern Expedition by the KMT-CCP coalition against the warlords begins.

1927   KMT leader Chiang Kai-shek attacks the CCP in the "White Terror" campaign. The First United Front breaks up. Chiang relocates China's capital to Nanjing. In August, the CCP-led Nanchang uprising leads to the creation of the Red Army.

1928   Mao Zedong and Zhu De unite to form the Jinggangshan base.

1929   The Jiangxi Soviet government carries out land reform. Chiang Kai-shek begins the "encirclement" campaigns against the CCP bases.

1931   Japan invades and occupies Northeast China (Manchuria); Japan later installs a Qing emperor there.

1934   The CCP military is forced into a strategic retreat by the KMT forces.

1935   In an enlarged CCP Politburo meeting in January, Mao Zedong emerges as a key leader of the CCP during the Long March.

1936   In the Xian incident in December, Chiang Kai-shek is kidnapped by his own generals and forced to stop civil war in order to prepare to fight against Japanese invasion. The CCP sends Zhou Enlai to Xian to help with negotiation that leads to Chiang's release. These events lead to the beginning of the Second United Front.

1937   The Japanese start a full-scale invasion of China. China's eight-year anti-Japanese war begins.

1941   Japan attacks Pearl Harbor. The United States enters the war. KMT-CCP military forces clash in Anhui Province.

1945   Japan surrenders unconditionally to the Allied powers. Cities are given to Chiang Kai-shek's army. Mao Zedong goes to Chongqing to negotiate with Chiang Kai-shek.

1946   Civil war between the CCP and the KMT breaks out.

1948   The People's Liberation Army (PLA) attacks KMT forces in north and central China.

1949   The People's Republic of China (PRC) is founded following the CCP defeat of KMT forces. Chairman Mao becomes the leader of the PRC, and Beijing is the capital. Chiang Kai-shek and the government of the Republic of China retreat to the island of Taiwan.

1950   The Sino-Soviet alliance is formed. China enters the Korean War to support North Korea. The Marriage Law and Agrarian Reform Law are promulgated. The PLA moves into Tibet.

1951   The Agreement of the Central People's Government and the Local Government of Tibet on Measures for the Peaceful Liberation of Tibet is signed. The agreement recognizes Tibet as part of China and grants the region autonomous status. Land reform continues to be carried out.

1952   The "Three-Anti" campaign is launched, targeting corruption, waste, and bureaucratism. The "Five-Anti" campaign is started to curb the violation of official regulations by private businesses.

1953   The First Five-Year Plan is launched. China follows the Soviet model of development that involves a centralized economy, the nationalization of industry and commerce, and the collectivization of agriculture. Joseph Stalin dies. The armistice ending the Korean War is signed in July.

1954   The first National People's Congress (NPC) meets and first PRC Constitution is promulgated. The NPC is the highest organ of state power. Regional leaders Gao Gang and Rao Shushi are purged for being pro-Soviet. Lower-stage agricultural co-ops are formed.

1955   Premier Zhou Enlai attends the Asian-African Conference in Bandung, Indonesia. Deng Xiaoping is elected to the Politburo. Higher-stage agricultural co-ops are formed.

1956   The Eighth CCP National Congress elects Mao Zedong party chairman; Liu Shaoqi, Zhou Enlai, Zhu De, and Chen Yun are elected vice chairmen; and Deng Xiaoping is elected secretary-general of the CCP. The "Hundred Flowers" campaign is launched. Mao invites criticism of the CCP's rule in order to shake up bureaucracy.

The antirightist campaign is launched. In reaction to the unexpectedly harsh criticism of the Hundred Flowers, the CCP strikes against critics. Many critics are "sent down."

1958   The Great Leap Forward is launched. One ambitious goal is to overtake Great Britain and catch up with the United States in the production of iron and steel. The people's communes are formed.

1959   Liu Shaoqi replaces Mao Zedong as president of the PRC, with Song Qingling and Dong Biwu as vice chairmen. Defense Minister Peng Dehuai criticizes the Great Leap Forward policy at the Lushan Conference. Peng Dehuai is purged. Lin Biao becomes defense minister. A revolt in Tibet is crushed. The Dalai Lama flees to exile in India.

1960   Sino-Soviet disputes become public. The Soviets notify China of their withdrawal of all technical personnel from China. Serious famine occurs across China in a post-Leap economic depression.

1961   The CCP Central Committee adopts economic adjustment policies. Mao Zedong retreats to the "second line" of leadership and turns economic policy over to Liu Shaoqi and Deng Xiaoping.

1962   In October and November, China and India fight a border war.

1963   Mao Zedong launches the socialist education movement.

1964   China carries out its first nuclear test.

1965   Yao Wenyuan publishes an article criticizing a play written by Wu Han. Yao denounces Wu's play *Hairui's Dismissal* as an "antiparty poisonous weed." Lin Biao publishes an article on "People's War."

1966   The "May 16 circular" marks the start of the Cultural Revolution. The Cultural Revolution Group is formed. The Red Guards emerge as Mao's mass ally in the Cultural Revolution and carry out a reign of terror against anyone and anything judged to be a remnant of capitalism or imperial China. PRC president Liu Shaoqi and CCP Secretary-General Deng Xiaoping are blamed as "capitalist roaders" and ousted from office.

1967   China explodes its first hydrogen bomb. The Cultural Revolution becomes more radical, and Red Guard factional coalitions violently clash.

1968   Mao Zedong sends the PLA to "support the left" and restore order in government offices, schools, and factories. Millions of young people are sent to the countryside to be reeducated by peasants. The campaign is called "up to the mountains and down to the countryside." The Soviet Union invades Prague, Czechoslovakia. China criticizes the Soviet Union as "socialist imperialism."

1969   China and the Soviet Union have several border clashes. Liu Shaoqi dies. The Ninth CCP National Congress is held. CCP vice chairman Lin Biao is designated as Mao's successor.

1970   China launches its first satellite. Party propaganda official Chen Boda is purged as a "sham Marxist."

1971   President Nixon's national security adviser Henry Kissinger visits China. The PRC is admitted to the United Nations (UN). Lin Biao dies in an airplane crash in Mongolia following an alleged coup to overthrow Mao, who had grown unhappy with Lin as his chosen successor.

1972   U.S. president Richard Nixon visits China in February. Nixon and Premier Zhou Enlai sign the Shanghai Communiqué, stating that there is but one China and that Taiwan is a part of China.

1973   The 10th CCP National Congress attempts to forge a new leadership. Deng Xiaoping is appointed vice premier. Commanders are shifted among military regions.

1974   Deng Xiaoping addresses the United Nations and explains the idea of the "Three Worlds." The First World refers to the United States and the Soviet Union; the Second World refers to Western Europe, Japan, and other developed countries; the Third World is the developing countries in Asia, Africa, and Latin America. Mao Zedong launches the "criticize Lin Biao and criticize Confucius" campaign. The radicals attempt to criticize Premier Zhou Enlai.

1975   Premier Zhou Enlai outlines the "four modernizations" at
the Fourth National People's Congress. As Zhou's health
declines, Deng Xiaoping takes more responsibility in managing state affairs. The struggle between the radicals and
more moderate CCP leaders intensifies.

1976   A huge earthquake in Tangshan kills more than 250,000
people. Zhou Enlai dies in January. Hua Guofeng is
appointed acting premier. A mass outpouring of mourning
for Zhou Enlai in Tiananmen turns into a protest against
the radical leaders. Deng Xiaoping is purged again following
the Tiananmen incident on April 5. Zhu De dies in July.
Mao Zedong dies in September. The radical group called
the "Gang of Four," led by Mao's wife, Jiang Qing, is
arrested in October. Hua Guofeng becomes the CCP chairman and chairman of the Central Military Commission.

1977   Deng Xiaoping returns to power. University admission based
on college entrance examinations start. The 11th CCP
National Congress calls an end to the Cultural Revolution.

1978   Deng gradually pushes Hua aside to become China's paramount leader, although he never assumes the top offices
himself. In December, the 3rd Plenum of the 11th CCP
Central Committee shifts the party's focus to modernization.
This is the beginning of reform and opening up.

1979   On January 1, the PRC and the United States establish diplomatic relations. Deng Xiaoping visits the United States.
China and Vietnam have a border clash. Special economic
zones are opened, including Shenzhen, Zhuhai, Shantou,
and Xiamen. The Democracy Wall movement calls for
greater political freedom but is suppressed. Deng puts forward the "four basic principles" emphasizing CCP leadership. The "rightists" are exonerated. Rural reforms,
including the agricultural household responsibility system,
are carried out.

1980   The CCP Central Committee rehabilitates Liu Shaoqi.
Zhao Ziyang, a loyal protégé of Deng Xiaoping, replaces

Hua Guofeng as premier. China joints the World Bank and the International Monetary Fund.

1981 Hu Yaobang replaces Hua Guofeng as chairman of the CCP Central Committee. Deng Xiaoping replaces Hua Guofeng as chairman of the Central Military Commission, thereby becoming the commander in chief of China's armed forces. The trial of the Gang of Four is held. The CCP issues the "Resolution on Certain Questions in the History of Our Party Since the Founding of the People's Republic of China." The resolution blames Mao's political and ideological mistakes for the disasters of the Great Leap Forward and the Cultural Revolution, but it concludes that his achievements far outweigh his shortcomings. Rural incomes are up amid urban shortages.

1982 The 12th CCP National Congress adopts new statutes. The title of the head of the CCP is changed to general secretary. The position of chairman of the CCP Central Committee is abolished. U.S. president Ronald Reagan visits Beijing. The August 27 Joint Communiqué agrees on fewer future U.S. weapons sales to Taiwan.

1983 The "anti-spiritual pollution" campaign stirs doubts in the CCP about reform, but the campaign ends soon.

1984 The CCP proposes new urban industrial reform measures. Fourteen coastal cities and the island of Hainan are opened to foreign investment. A Sino-British joint declaration regarding Hong Kong's return to China is signed.

1985 Many old cadres retire. Mikhail Gorbachev becomes the top leader in the Soviet Union.

1986 The Shanghai stock market reopens for the first time since 1949. Students protest in major cities, demanding more political reform.

1987 Student demonstrations are suppressed. Hu Yaobang is forced to resign as general secretary because he is said to be too sympathetic to students and intellectuals calling for more democracy. Zhao Ziyang replaces Hu as general secretary of the CCP. Li Peng succeeds Zhao as premier. The 13th CCP National Congress favors continued economic and political reforms.

1988   Hainan is approved for provincial status. Inflation is up. Price reform is aborted. Economic austerity begins.

1989   Soviet leader Mikhail Gorbachev visits China to normalize relations between the two countries. Hu Yaobang dies on April 15. Students gather in Tiananmen Square to pay their respects to Hu Yaobang, regarded by many as a political reformer. The student gathering turns into a mass demonstration against corruption and for democracy. Broad popular protests are followed by repression and martial law. Zhao Ziyang is removed from power by Deng Xiaoping. Jiang Zemin becomes the general secretary of the CCP. Jiang also succeeds Deng Xiaoping as chairman of the Central Military Commission.

1990   The hard-liners gain influence in the leadership. Many reform policies are put on hold.

1991   Economic austerity continues. The collapse of the Soviet Union further alarms China's leaders. Deng Xiaoping concludes that the Soviet collapse is not because of reform but the lack of timely reform.

1992   Deng Xiaoping's southern tour promotes deep reform and comprehensive opening. Economic austerity ends. The 14th CCP National Congress approves renewed economic reform.

1993   The 3rd Plenum of the 14th CCP Congress adopts the document "Establishment of a Socialist Market Economic System." Jiang Zemin succeeds Yang Shangkun as president of the PRC.

1994   The Three Gorges Dam project starts. Inflation is high. Popular discontent grows.

1995   Senior leader Chen Yun dies. Beijing strongly reacts to Taiwanese leader Li Teng-hui's visit to the United States.

1996   The economy stabilizes. The Taiwan crisis escalates as the PLA conducts missile exercises.

1997   The 15th CCP National Congress proposes significant advances for economic reform. Deng Xiaoping dies at age 93. President Jiang Zemin visits the United States. Hong Kong returns to Chinese sovereignty after nearly 150 years as a British colony.

1998   At the Ninth National People's Congress, Zhu Rongji succeeds Li Peng as premier. Zhu unveils a dramatic package of reform. The Asian financial crisis negatively affects China. China maintains the value of the yuan and provides assistance to other Asian nations. U.S. president Bill Clinton visits China.

1999   In May, the NATO bombing of the Chinese embassy in Belgrade, Yugoslavia, sparks a crisis in Sino-American relations. In November, China and the United States agree to the terms of China's World Trade Organization entry. In December, Portugal returns Macao to China, ending 442 years of colonial rule.

2000   A new five-year economic and social plan calls for relatively rapid economic development while improving qualitative aspects of growth. Chen Shui-bian of the Democratic Progressive Party wins Taiwan's presidency, putting the Nationalist Party out of power on Taiwan for the first time.

2001   Tensions in China-U.S. relations are high as the result of a U.S. spy plane and Chinese fighter jet collision. After the September 11 terrorist attacks on the United States, China cooperates with the United States in the fight against terrorism. China hosts the Asia-Pacific Economic Cooperation (APEC) meeting. President George W. Bush attends the APEC meeting in Shanghai. China becomes a member of the World Trade Organization.

2002   The 16th CCP National Congress results in leadership transition. Hu Jintao succeeds Jiang Zemin as the general secretary of the CCP Central Committee.

2003   The 10th National People's Congress is held. Hu Jintao succeeds Jiang Zemin as president of the PRC. Wen Jiabao succeeds Zhu Rongji as premier. Hu and Wen take decisive measures against the severe acute respiratory syndrome (SARS) health crisis.

2004   Jiang Zemin steps down from his last position as chairman of the Central Military Commission. Hu Jintao further consolidates his power as the top party, state, and military leader.

2005   Hu Jintao stresses sustainability and social equity rather than gross domestic product (GDP) growth. The new slogan is "harmonious society."

2006   Politburo member and Shanghai party secretary Chen Liangyu is removed from his post on charges of corruption. The CCP Central Committee discusses building a harmonious society.

2007   The 17th CCP National Congress adopts Hu's idea of the "scientific outlook on development." Hu is reelected general secretary of the CCP Central Committee. A new party leadership is elected, including young Politburo Standing Committee members Xi Jinping and Li Keqiang.

2008   In May a massive earthquake hits Sichuan. Unrest occurs in Tibet and is suppressed. In August, the Summer Olympic Games are held in Beijing. In response to the global financial crisis, China announces an economy stimulus package of $586 billion. Ma Ying-jeou regains Taiwan's presidency for the Nationalist Party, calling for improved relations with mainland China.

2009   The 4th Plenum of the 17th CCP Central Committee discusses enhancing intraparty democracy. Large-scale unrest occurs in Xinjiang and is forcefully suppressed. In November, U.S. president Barack Obama visits China.

2010   At the NPC meeting in March, Premier Wen Jiabao highlights the need to boost spending and redistribute wealth. The World Expo is held in Shanghai. Xi Jinping is appointed vice chairman of the Central Military Commission, which is a significant step in leadership transition.

2011   President Hu Jintao visits the United States in January. Hu and President Obama issue a joint statement calling for a cooperative, positive, and comprehensive relationship between China and the United States.

2012   The 18th CCP National Congress will be held and a new leadership is to emerge.

Map of China. (Cartography by Bookcomp, Inc.)

Chapter 1

Historical Overview: From Revolutions to Reforms

CHINA'S CULTURE AND POLITICAL TRADITION

China has a long history and rich cultural tradition. During the Spring and Autumn and Warring States periods, a hundred schools of thinking flourished in China. Among them, the most prominent schools of thinking included Confucianism, Daoism, and legalism. From the first emperor who united China under the Qin dynasty in 221 BCE to the collapse of the Manchu regime in the Qing dynasty in 1911, the Chinese imperial system lasted over two millennia.

The first united dynasty, Qin, was short lived, partially because of its excessive use of force and heavy reliance on punishment promoted by legalism. In the second dynasty, West Han, Emperor Wudi promoted Confucianism as the official learning. Confucius emphasized the value of education, family, harmony, social order, and respect for authority.

Legalism stressed the absolute rule of the emperor and strong order and discipline. While Confucianism promotes self-cultivation and education, legalists believe that the threat of punishment will work better than moral teaching to enforce people's compliance with the imperial rule. The Chinese traditional political system was strongly influenced by both Confucianism and legalism. Almost all the major dynasties after Han emphasized both moral teaching as well as maintaining order by force.

The gentry system, in which the official-scholar-landlord dominated China's politics and economics, was deeply rooted and long lasting. Key elements of the system included an imperial court, a system of meritocracy based on imperial examination, and landlord elites. "The

The Great Wall of China is one of the largest structures in the world. The wall began when a series of smaller structures was linked during the Qin dynasty in the third century BCE, and it eventually extended over roughly 4,000 miles of northern China, from the Bohai Sea in the east to the Uighur region in the west. (Corel.)

intelligentsia, members of the state bureaucracy and landowners formed a close-knit social class known as the gentry, which exercised robust hegemony over all the important levers of economic, political, and social power."[1] Traditional Chinese elites believed that farming was the foundation of the economy and commerce must be regulated by the state. Landholding was considered true wealth. The strong focus on landholding might be one of the reasons why China did not develop a Western-style capitalist system. The imperial examination system focused on learning and interpreting the Confucian classics. When the best and brightest of successive generations of Chinese youth were devoted to excelling on the official exams, scientific and technological innovations were often ignored. That fact might be another explanation for why China did not experience industrialization as early as Western Europe did. Another possible explanation for China's late industrialization might be China's huge population. With a large and rapidly growing population, the Chinese might have felt less demand for developing labor-saving technologies than the Europeans.

As Western Europe and North America underwent industrialization in the 19th century, they quickly surpassed China in productivity and in military technology. As a latecomer to modernization, China learned the bitter lessons of backwardness in the "century of humiliation," from the Opium War during 1839–1842 to the establishment of the People's Republic of China in 1949.

THE 1911 REVOLUTION

China in the beginning of the 20th century was confronting a total crisis. The key question was who could save the country. What path would lead to the survival and then the rise of China? Many root causes of the successes and failures of China's modernization can be found in the pre-1949-era struggle for national salvation and social revolution.

The Qing dynasty (1644–1911) first experienced revitalization and later suffered a systemic crisis. In the 18th century, China was a strong nation with the largest gross domestic product (GDP) in the world, accounting for about one-third of global output. The crisis of the late Qing era resulted from a combination of internal decay and foreign aggression. Chinese dynasties would normally go through cycles of rise and fall. By the late 19th century and early 20th century, the Qing dynasty was in sharp decline. Traditionally, most external challenges to China's security came from the nomadic people from the north. The Qing rulers were caught by surprise when the British navy attacked China's southern coast in 1839. Following the Opium War (1839–1842), China was repeatedly defeated by imperialist powers.

From 1851 to1864, a large-scale peasant rebellion led to the establishment of the Taiping Tianguo (Heavenly Kingdom of Great Peace) in southern China. The confrontation between the Qing army and the peasant rebels resulted in enormous loss of human life and huge material destruction. Although the peasant rebellion was finally suppressed by the Qing military, the legitimacy and resources of the Qing leadership came under severe strain.

The most severe and shocking foreign challenge came from the Japanese military in the Sino-Japanese War (1894–1895). It was particularly humiliating that the huge Qing empire was defeated by a much smaller but better-organized, better-equipped, and newly modernized Japan. This was a huge wake-up call for the Chinese. Japan's success in the conflict was a result of its successful modernization through the Meiji Restoration beginning in 1868. The Japanese reformers built an effective central government, a modern military based on conscription rather than reliant on the traditional samurai, and a modern education system. Most impressively, Japan was able to build a strong foundation for its industry in a short period of time. China's open-minded intellectuals, such as Kang Youwei and Liang Qichao, attempted to reform China following the example of Japan. Unfortunately, the conservative forces in the Qing court defeated the "hundred days of reform" effort in 1898.

In 1900, the Boxer Uprising surged to expel foreign influence in China. The Qing court first encouraged the Boxers. The Boxers attacked Western missionaries and diplomats. Such attacks led to a forceful joint foreign intervention. After the bloody suppression of the Boxers by the Western army, the Qing government was forced to pay the vast indemnity of 450 million taels to the Western powers.

Sun Yat-sen was a revolutionary who gave voice to vigorous anti-Manchu and prorepublican attitudes, and he maintained a hope for developing the institutions to make China a strong modern state. According to Sun, the worldwide trend of moving toward a republican form of government was unstoppable. Countries following the trend would be prosperous, and countries going against the trend would perish. Sun organized the Revolutionary Alliance. Sun's views were fundamentally nationalist and republican, although elements of socialism were present too. Sun consistently sought the overthrow of Qing rule with armed force. Between 1906 and 1908, the Revolutionary Alliance directed several unsuccessful uprisings against the Qing government.

By the summer of 1911, the number of active Revolutionary Alliance members had grown from around 400 in 1905 to almost 10,000. In October 1911, a revolutionary uprising took place in Wuchang city in central China. Sun learned about the October 1911 Wuchang uprising when he was in the United States, and he traveled to London and Paris to gain European support before returning to China. When he returned to China in late December 1911, Sun was elected by the delegates from 16 provincial assemblies as "provisional president" of the Republic of China.

Sun assumed office in Nanjing on January 1, 1912, inaugurating the Republic of China. The harsh reality is that Sun did not have enough military or political power to lead a head-to-head confrontation with the Qing military under Gen. Yuan Shikai. As a compromise, Sun offered the leadership position of the republic to Yuan if Yuan would force the abdication of the Qing emperor. Following the abdication of the boy emperor Puyi on February 12, 1912, Yuan Shikai became the president of the new republic. The dream of building a new republic collapsed quickly, because Yuan was neither willing nor able to build a republic. On the contrary, Yuan tried to build a new dynasty with himself as the emperor.

The revolutionary forces and the mobilized public were not willing to turn back the clock of history. They staged nationwide protests and resistance against Yuan's attempt to return to an imperial system. Frustrated in his ill-designed attempt, Yuan died in 1916. With Yuan's demise, China entered a period of warlord politics, political insecurity, and intellectual self-scrutiny and exploration.

MAY FOURTH MOVEMENT AND THE NATIONALIST REVOLUTION

It was during the era of internal crisis and foreign threat that China experienced a new cultural movement. In 1915, Chen Duxiu founded the *New Youth* magazine in Shanghai, promoting democracy and science and criticizing feudal dictatorship and feudal rituals. In 1917, the enlightened and open-minded educator Cai Yuanpei became the president of Peking University. Cai promoted educational reform and education renewal. He invited Chen Duxiu to serve as dean of liberal arts at Peking University and bring *New Youth* to Beijing.

During World War I, China sent laborers to work for the Allies. More than 2,000 Chinese workers died in France. After the war ended, the Chinese people had high expectations for their delegation to the postwar treaty negotiations at Versailles. The Chinese delegation was surprised to find that early in 1917, in return for Japanese naval assistance against the Germans, Great Britain, France, and Italy had signed a secret treaty ensuring support of Japan's claims regarding the disposal of Germany's rights in China's Shandong Province after the war. In April 1919, U.S. president Woodrow Wilson agreed with David Lloyd George of Britain and Georges Clemenceau of France to transfer all of Germany's Shandong rights to Japan in the Treaty of Versailles. When the news reached Beijing, it triggered mass protests in Tiananmen on

May 4, 1919, which were followed by demonstrations in cities all over China.

The May Fourth protesters were motivated by nationalism. They searched hard for the causes of China's backwardness and national humiliation. The most important and enduring slogan of the May Fourth Movement was "Democracy and Science." Chinese students believed that the lack of science and democracy led to China's backwardness. This call for democracy and science is still relevant today. The May Fourth Movement has two broad aspects: On the political front, May Fourth was an anti-imperialism, antifeudalism, prodemocratic, and nationalist salvation movement. On the cultural front, May Fourth is considered a new cultural movement with two key components, that is, Chen Duxiu's *New Youth* thought liberation movement and Cai Yuanpei's educational reform movement at Peking University.

Li Dazhao, a professor at Peking University, actively promoted Marxism and revolutionary culture. With assistance from the Comintern, Li and Chen Duxiu became the key founders of the Chinese Communist Party (CCP) in 1921. Mao Zedong participated in the founding conference of the CCP. At the meeting, Chen was elected the first general secretary of the CCP.

The May Fourth Movement prepared political leaders that strongly influenced China's political change. Following the new cultural movement, a generation of Chinese revolutionary youths studied and worked in Europe. This group included Zhou Enlai, Deng Xiaoping, and Zhu De, who later became critical leaders in Chinese revolution and construction.

Sun Yat-sen searched many sources for international support for Chinese revolution. In the end, he found support from the Soviet Union. Under the urging of Soviet advisers, Sun's Nationalist Party (Kuomintang or KMT) and the CCP formed the First United Front in 1924. Sun's untimely death in 1925 prevented him from implementing his three principles of the people, calling for democracy, nationalism, and people's livelihood. Chiang Kai-shek emerged as a key military and political leader of the KMT. Under the First United Front, the revolutionary army with Chiang as commander undertook a successful northern expedition against the warlords. Fundamental differences between the KMT and CCP, however, led to a bloody split when the Nationalist forces seized Shanghai, the largest city in China.

Nationalist leader Chiang Kai-shek gave orders to violently suppress the Communists. Thousands of CCP members were murdered, and CCP organizations in the cities were driven underground. Meanwhile, CCP leaders Mao Zedong, Zhu De, and others called for armed uprisings against Chiang Kai-shek. They created revolutionary bases and conducted guerrilla warfare against the KMT in Jiangxi Province.

Chiang Kai-shek conducted several rounds of military campaigns aimed at suppressing the CCP forces. In 1934, the Red Army under the CCP leadership was forced into retreat. That retreat was the beginning of the legendary Long March that lasted for a whole year. When the Long March began, the central Red Army was 100,000 soldiers strong. When the Long March ended a year later, only about 5,000 of them had survived. It is significant that the CCP core leadership survived the Long March, with Mao Zedong rising to a dominant position. The Long March generation, including Deng Xiaoping, dominated CCP politics until the early 1990s.

THE ANTI-JAPANESE WAR

Japan's success in modernization and its victory against China in 1895 and against Russia in 1905 led to the dramatic rise of military and imperialistic ambitions. After its colonization of Korea in 1910, Japan was aimed at total domination of East Asia. When Japan invaded and occupied Northeast China (Manchuria) in 1931, and especially when Japan began its comprehensive invasion of China in 1937, the very survival of China as an independent nation came under clear and present danger.

Nationalist leader Chiang Kai-shek perceived the Chinese Communists as his top threat. He carried out a policy of suppressing the CCP before confronting the Japanese aggressors. In December 1936, Chiang was preparing a final assault on the CCP when he flew to Xian to persuade his regional commanders Zhang Xueliang and Yang Hucheng to attack the Red Army. Unwilling to fight fellow Chinese and eager to fight against the Japanese invaders, Generals Zhang and Yang arrested Chiang in order to persuade him to stop the civil war and to defend China against Japan. The dramatic arrest of Chiang in the Xian incident in December 1936 facilitated the rise of the Second United Front. CCP leader Zhou Enlai went to Xian to help with the negotiation. In the end, Chiang was allowed to fly back to the capital, Nanjing, after he agreed to stop fighting against the CCP and prepare to fight against the Japanese invaders.

The international context for the rise of the Second United Front included a Soviet factor and then an American factor. The Soviet Union did not want to confront the German threat on the west and the Japanese threat on the east. Stalin urged the CCP to form the Second United Front with the KMT to confront the Japanese threat. This would reduce pressure by the Japanese military on the Soviet Union.

The U.S. factor also helped to strengthen the Second United Front. President Franklin D. Roosevelt saw the Japanese imperialistic and militaristic policy in China and the Asia-Pacific region as a threat to American interests. The American people were sympathetic to the Chinese as victims of Japanese invasion. The Flying Tigers (volunteer fighter pilots) from the United States began helping the Chinese with air defense even before the U.S. declaration of war against Japan, following the vicious surprise Japanese attack on Pearl Harbor. When the United States officially joined the war against Japan and became a major player in the international alliance against fascist powers, China's Second United Front became a key part of the international alliance of the United States, the Soviet Union, Great Britain, and China against Japan and Germany. The United States provided material support and military advice to the KMT government. The CCP warmly welcomed American observers to Yanan and other CCP areas. The United States helped to strengthen the Second United Front in China. When Japan surrendered, the United States tried to bring the CCP and KMT to the negotiation table to form a coalition government.

If May Fourth represents the birth of modern Chinese nationalism, then the anti-Japanese war period led to the maturity of Chinese nationalism. For the first time, the majority of the Chinese were united in a joint fight for national salvation.

The KMT and the CCP cooperated against Japanese invasion in the Second United Front, but they also continued their struggle against each other. Mutual suspicion and frequent friction occurred between the KMT and the CCP forces.

While the KMT forces under Chiang were dealing with the Japanese forces on the front battlefield, the CCP forces were able to mobilize and expand quickly in the Japanese-occupied areas. The anti-Japanese war provided the CCP with an unprecedented opportunity to grow militarily and politically. The People's Republic of China (PRC) official history used to describe the KMT as only interested in civil war and very passive about resisting Japan. In reality, the KMT did confront a significant portion of the Japanese forces. If the Japanese had not had to confront the Nationalist military and had been able to concentrate most of their forces on attacking the CCP forces, the CCP might have had a much tougher time in its guerilla warfare strategy against the Japanese.

From 1937 to 1945, the CCP grew from a party that was almost destroyed by the KMT at the end of the legendary Long March to a formidable force of 1 million party members and 1 million battlefield-tested soldiers. That growth set the stage for a tough, bloody confrontation between the CCP and the KMT forces.

Chinese history might be quite different without the anti-Japanese war. The Pacific war between the United States and Japan and the U.S. atomic bombings of Hiroshima and Nagasaki had profound impact on the war against Japan, speeding up Japan's unconditional surrender in August 1945.

China sacrificed more than any other nation in the international fight against Japanese militarism. Over 30 million Chinese died in the anti-Japanese war. The war, on one hand, further exposed China's weaknesses facing a powerful aggressor. On the other hand, the anti-Japanese war greatly promoted Chinese nationalism and national coherence. When Japan surrendered unconditionally to the Allied powers, the unequal treaties against China ended. It was at the end of World War II that China emerged as one of the "big five" powers (United States, Soviet Union, United Kingdom, France, and China) and a permanent member of the Security Council of the newly founded United Nations.

China's position in the world was enhanced as a victor of World War II. However, the country was deeply divided between the KMT- and CCP-occupied areas. In August 1945, U.S. ambassador Patrick Hurley escorted Mao Zedong from Yanan to Chongqing (the wartime capital of the Nationalist government) for negotiations with Chiang Kai-shek. The talks continued until October 10, 1945. The two sides reached a tentative agreement for building a coalition government. At that time, there was still hope that the Second United Front might survive in a coalition government. When the U.S.-sponsored peace efforts between the KMT and CCP collapsed in 1946, the stage was set for a final battle between the two parties.

When national salvation became the top priority during the war against Japan, the enlightenment and democratic elements of the new culture movement were left as back banners. China did not have an opportunity to experience gradual growth of democratic institutions.

THE CIVIL WAR AND COMMUNIST REVOLUTION

Chiang Kai-shek and Mao Zedong represented two lines of China's development and China's future. From 1927 to 1949, with an intermission of the anti-Japanese United Front, from 1937 to 1945, the KMT under Chiang and the CCP under Mao struggled to control China's destiny. In the end, Mao's way prevailed against Chiang because of the following factors.

First, Mao was a true nationalist. In the eyes of many Chinese, the Nationalist party was not nationalistic enough. A section of the former KMT under Wang Jingwei surrendered to Japan and formed a puppet regime. Chiang was a nationalist. But in the eyes of some Chinese nationalists, there was no one who could better represent the national interests of China than Mao. It was the CCP that was most active in the Japanese-occupied areas, organizing guerrilla warfare against the Japanese. The KMT government did engage in resistance against Japan. But a widespread perception was that Chiang was more devoted to civil war than fighting against foreign enemies.

Second, Mao was able to clearly articulate a line that provided hope to a majority of the Chinese people. Adapting Marxism to China's unique conditions, Mao emphasized the alliance of workers and peasants. Considering the fact that the majority of Chinese people were farmers, Mao classified the poor and low-middle-class peasants as the main revolutionary forces. Instead of promoting the bookish Bolshevism, as Wang Ming and other Soviet-trained Chinese communists did, Mao consistently emphasized that Marxism must be adapted to Chinese special conditions. Mao's line was a "new democracy" (*xin minzhu zhuyi*) in which the peasants, workers, would be the masters. At the same time, intellectuals and nationalist industrialists and merchants would all make positive contributions to building a "free, democratic, prosperous, and strong new China" (*ziyou, minzhu, fuqiang de xin zhongguo*). This idealist vision motivated millions of people to devote themselves to the CCP cause.

Third, the CCP developed strong organization with tough discipline. The CCP under Mao became better organized than any other political force in China. The party had very strong discipline based on the Leninist organizational principle of democratic centralism, which is democratic in style and centralist in essence. The power of organization was developed to a height under Mao. Sun Yat-sen once said that the Chinese are like a pan of loose sands. That was a key reason of Chinese weakness. The CCP was able to first organize itself and then develop effective channels to organize China.[2]

Fourth, Mao paid special attention to the critical role of the military. One of Mao's most famous slogans was "Political power comes from the barrel of a gun." Chiang Kai-shek also believed in the power of the military. But as a professional soldier-turned-general and dictator, Chiang did not fully appreciate that the guns must be controlled by the party. Effective political control of the guns was one of the tools that helped the CCP to defeat Chiang.

Finally and perhaps most significantly, the CCP was able to use the united front strategy. The First United Front allowed the CCP to grow in its coalition with the KMT against the warlords. The Second United Front gave the CCP an unprecedented opportunity to expand into the Japanese-occupied areas of China. Even after the open split with the KMT, the CCP was still able to develop a broad united front including all positive forces that could be mobilized for its causes. With this strategy, Mao was able to use all talents available for the CCP's struggle, first against the Japanese and then against the KMT. With the united front policy, the CCP was able to maximize support and minimize fears. Thus, the Second United Front strategy was critical for the success of national salvation and social revolution.

Let us briefly examine the positive and negative aspects of the revolutionary legacy. On the positive side, the revolution destroyed the old regime that was keeping China weak and backward. The revolution greatly promoted Chinese nationalism and national coherence. For the first time in a long period, China's mainland was truly unified. That unification made it possible to build a national political and economic system. The PRC government was able to extend the power of the political center to every major region of China. The united front strategy was successful in mobilizing broad support for the CCP's rise to power. The revolution destroyed the old treaty port system and changed China's semicolonial status. The Chinese people stood up in the sense that no foreign country could impose its will on China. The revolution provided a new vision for China's future. Widespread despair was replaced by great popular hope for a bright future. The revolution created a new source of legitimacy. A new civil order replaced decades of chaos and violence. This civil order was absolutely essential for the rise of China.

On the negative side, the total crisis led to an overcentralized political system. Party-military-state power was highly centralized. Total crisis resulted in a totalist regime. Even today, China is still confronting the tough tasks of separating the party from the state. Mao's victory led to strong charisma and later resulted in a personality cult. The lack of rational-legal restraint of leadership power caused a systemic crisis. Leadership succession arrangements under Mao all failed badly (Liu Shaoqi, Lin Biao, Wang Hongwen, and Hua Guofeng). Although Hua obtained all top titles of the party, state, and military leadership, he was able to hold onto power only for two years. The lifetime tenure system became a serious issue under Mao. It was not until the end of the Deng Xiaoping era that the lifetime party-state leadership system was finally changed. The revolution uprooted the traditional social fabrics without leaving room for the growth of a civil society. The military-style governance led to heavy reliance on commands and plan and not enough on individual initiatives. Mao Zedong first obtained control of the CCP-led military in 1935. He remained the chairman of the Central Military Commission until his death. The politicization of the military, especially during the Cultural Revolution, had negative consequences for developing a healthy civil-military relation.

The military and political victory of the CCP over the KMT during 1946–1949 completed China's social revolution. The rise of the Cold War, with growing tensions between the Soviet Union and the United States, led to strong U.S. distrust of the CCP. When the United States strengthened support to the KMT, Chiang thought that he could launch a decisive battle to defeat the CCP in a short period of time. It was Chiang's overconfidence and hasty military action that caused the quick demise of the KMT government. The KMT lost power so quickly because it was not able to conduct the land reform demanded by millions of peasants. As a defender of the landlords, the KMT put itself on the opposing side of the peasants, who overwhelmingly supported the CCP. In the cities, the KMT government was not able to control widespread corruption and hyperinflation. Official corruption and inflation destroyed the legitimacy of the regime. On the cultural front, the KMT government carried out oppressive policies that caused strong resistance from both left-wing intellectuals and a majority of the students. Finally, the KMT military was so busy occupying the cities that it ignored the large countryside. As a result, the CCP was able to mobilize peasant support and successfully carried out a strategy of "surrounding the cities from the countryside." In a predominately peasant society like China, whoever controlled the countryside finally was able to control the whole country. By 1949, the CCP was able to gain control of most parts of China. Chiang Kai-shek was forced to fly to Taiwan.

MAO ZEDONG AND THE NEW DEMOCRACY

In June 1949, Mao Zedong issued his speech "On the people's democratic dictatorship." The essence of the "New Democracy" would be the "people's democratic dictatorship." The Second United Front came to an end when the CCP-KMT civil war broke out in 1946. The New Democracy was a motivating vision against the corrupt and authoritarian KMT. The CCP inaugurated not a "proletariat dictatorship" but a "new democracy," which promised a useful role to all patriotic classes in implementing a progressive but relatively moderate social program.

The New Democracy was supposed to be democracy for the people against the "people's enemies." The "people" referred to a democratic alliance of workers, peasants, petty bourgeoisie, and "national bourgeoisie." "People's enemies" referred to big landlords; capitalists who had close connections with the KMT regime; national traitors who worked on behalf of the Japanese and other imperialists; officials in the KMT government, military, and security agencies; and other "counterrevolutionary" elements.

The Chinese People's Political Consultative Conference (CPPCC) was the new organ used by the CCP to promote its national agenda. In September 1949 the CPPCC passed the Organic Law of the Central People's Government and the Common Program. The Common

Program was a provisional constitution. The hallmark of the Common Program was gradualism.

The Marriage Law was passed in 1950. That law abolished traditional arranged marriages and other forms of discrimination against women. It stated that the foundation of a marriage should be love and mutual respect between the husband and wife. The Agrarian Reform Law was also passed in 1950. Under the new law, land reform proper was launched. The major steps were a class identification of all village inhabitants, followed by the confiscation and redistribution of landlord land and other productive property. The work teams sent by the government to the countryside sought to mobilize entire villages against the landlords through such devices as "speak bitterness" meetings and mass trials. More than 1 million landlords were executed during the land reform.

The land reform was completed by 1953, except in areas belonging to ethnic minorities. About half of all the arable land changed hands, and 300 million peasants became independent holders of small pieces of farmland. Between 1949 and 1953, about 56 percent of China's farmland was redistributed to 60–70 percent of all peasant households; of the land that changed ownership, two-thirds came from landlords and less than one-third from rich peasants. In the redistribution, less than two-thirds of the land went to poor peasants, while over one-third went to middle peasants. The net effect was to break the power of the landlord class to the benefit of the poor and middle-class peasants. Land reform was very popular among the peasants. It helped to consolidate CCP control of the countryside. It destroyed traditional gentry power in rural China. The old rural elites were stripped of their economic assets, and as a class the landlords were humiliated.

From 1950 to 1957, the new PRC government obtained far-reaching popular support as a result of its achievements in securing social order, controlling inflation, launching economic development, improving living conditions, and restoring national pride.

The New Democracy (1949–1953) was an idealistic and practical direction. It was inspiring and attractive to a large number of people. It provided great hope to the revolutionaries and the progressive public in the new People's Republic. Unfortunately, a lot of moderate ideas of the New Democracy were pushed aside in a hasty transition to socialism. A "general line of constructing socialism" soon replaced the initial ideas of gradual transition.

During the period from 1949 to 1957, broad agreement existed within the CCP leadership on adopting the Soviet model of socialism. Over time, there was much discussion over what were the positive and negative features of the Soviet model. The CCP had to decide how to adapt the model to suit Chinese conditions. Mao Zedong's discontent with the Soviet model and search for an alternative led to the Great Leap Forward and, later, the Cultural Revolution.

In the beginning of the PRC, there were two important external events. One was the signing of the Sino-Soviet Treaty of Friendship, Alliance, and Mutual Assistance on February 14, 1950. The treaty was an indication of China's leaning toward the Soviet Union in the Cold War. The other important event was the Korean War (1950–1953). This war intensified the Cold War confrontation in Asia and created more hostility between China and the United States. It was largely responsible for the lack of normal relations between China and the United States for nearly three decades.

In 1953 the First Five-Year Plan was launched, and the "general line for the transition to socialism" was introduced. The plan, based on Soviet experience and advice, was strongly weighted in favor of the development of heavy industry. The investment distribution reflected this bias: industry received 58.2 percent; transportation and communication, 19.2 percent; and agriculture, 7.6 percent. The result was a dramatic growth in industrial output. For instance, steel output rose from 1.4 million tons in 1952 to 5.24 million tons in 1957. But agriculture lagged far behind, with an annual growth rate of about 3 percent, just about keeping pace with the annual population growth of about 2.2 percent.

The First Five-Year Plan was a success, revitalizing agriculture while forging ahead with industrialization to achieve overall economic growth rates (particularly in industry) without precedent. At the same time, socialization of the means of production was achieved in both agriculture and industry, expediting the transition to socialism in unexpectedly short order.

In retrospect, China might have been able to do better if the New Democracy era lasted longer and there was no rush to socialist transition. This, however, was not realistic because of Mao's utopian vision and revolutionary drive to push China onto the socialist road as soon as possible. The transitional stage initially was estimated to take about 15 years. In reality, the much shorter transition had a heavy cost.

In 1954, the PRC Constitution was adopted. It established the fundamental framework of the PRC political system. Mao pushed hard for agricultural cooperation. First, the government encouraged villagers to form "mutual-aid teams." By the end of 1953, 43 percent of the peasants were in mutual-aid teams of four or five families. Soon the Agricultural Producers' Cooperatives (APCs) of 20 to 30 families emerged and developed from lower level to higher level by increasing the nature of the collective economy. By 1957, over 90 percent of the peasants were in higher cooperatives.

In 1956 Mao put forward the "ten great relationships," which promoted a new line in economic development. Mao provided some rational analysis of key issues in the Chinese economy. But unfortunately, many good ideas about the ten relationships were not put into practice.

On the political front, a major event was the antirightist campaign of 1957. Initially Mao Zedong encouraged the intellectuals to speak out and allow a "hundred flowers" to bloom. When the criticism of government work turned harsher than expected, Mao launched a political campaign against the so-called anti-CCP "rightists." The impact on China's intellectuals was devastating. About 550,000 intellectuals were labeled rightists. Most intellectuals were afraid of speaking the truth as a result of the harshness of the movement. The so-called New Democracy turned out to be less democratic but more dictatorial.

THE GREAT LEAP FORWARD

The second session of the Eighth CCP National Congress, held in Beijing in May 1958, officially endorsed the Great Leap Forward (GLF). The "three red flags" of the "general line," the people's communes, and the GLF became dominant themes during 1958–1959. The people's communes were designed to be the nation's basic social units as well as organizations of agricultural and industrial production. They were also to be the Chinese alternative to the Western route to modernization that Mao rejected.

What were the main causes of the Great Leap Forward? Mao pushed the GLF as an alternative to the Soviet model. Main elements of the GLF strategy called for the country (1) to make up for a lack of capital in both industry and agriculture by fully mobilizing underemployed labor power; (2) to carry out "planning" by setting ambitious goals for

China's leading economic sectors and encouraging other sectors to catch up with these key sectors; (3) to rely on both modern and traditional methods to enhance output in industry; and (4) in all areas, to disregard technical norms in favor of, in the lexicon of the times, achieving "more, faster, better, and more economical results." In practice, the "more and faster" overwhelmed the "better and more economical."[3]

What were the main mistakes of the GLF? China's economic balance was seriously damaged by the overemphasis on the production of iron and steel. Political mobilization ignored the natural laws of economics. Blind pursuit of a higher level of ownership in the people's communes severely disrupted agricultural production. Farmers were forced to give up family farming and rushed into the people's communes. Under political pressure, leaders at different levels exaggerated economic output.

By 1960, the GLF had produced economic disaster in the hinterland. Famine was stalking the land, and soon the economic malaise spread throughout the cities. A massive famine caused at least 20 million deaths.

What is the legacy of the GLF? The Leap was a catastrophic failure. Instead of reflecting seriously on his mistakes, Mao tried to blame the following factors for the bad results of the "three difficult years" (1959–1962): natural disaster, antiparty forces, and Soviet withdrawal of technical experts and aid at the height of the 1960 crisis. The collapse of the Leap affected the CCP's reputation in two ways. First, it impaired the prestige of the party as a whole among the masses. Second, it damaged Mao's personal reputation for infallibility among the party elite.[4]

THE CULTURAL REVOLUTION

What were the fundamental causes of the Cultural Revolution? In order to understand the origins of the Cultural Revolution, one must understand Mao's reactions to a complex mix of domestic and foreign developments over the decade preceding its launch. Mao had a strong passion for "continuing revolution." Ideology and policy conflicts between China and the Soviet Union also had profound effects on Mao's thinking and behavior.

After Nikita Khrushchev criticized the mistakes of Joseph Stalin at the 20th Congress of the Soviet Communist Party, Mao thought Khrushchev betrayed Stalin. Mao developed an obsession with revisionism and the possibility of the emergence of a Khrushchev-like figure in China. CCP leaders began to criticize Soviet foreign policy in 1960. By 1962 the Sino-Soviet differences were aired openly, and mutual attacks became more bitter. Mao's antirevisionist international stand had a strong bearing on his approach to internal politics. PRC president Liu Shaoqi was criticized later as "China's Khrushchev." Mao thought that Liu Shaoqi represented a "revisionist line" that threatened the "continuing revolution."

Mao also attacked PRC president Liu Shaoqi and CCP general secretary Deng Xiaoping as "capitalist roaders." In Mao's view, Liu and Deng were undermining his power and authority in the party and state. Mao gained the ideological high ground by attacking capitalist tendency, but he lost touch with China's reality, which was at the early stage of the socialist construction. China indeed needed some "capitalist measures" to develop its economy. Mao was not willing or able to accept this. To Mao, "public" was better than "private," because communism was superior to capitalism.

On May 16, 1966, a document (drafted by Mao) was issued in the name of the CCP Central Committee for circulation. The "May 16 circular" became the programmatic document of the Cultural Revolution. The new Central Cultural Revolution Group (CCRG) was placed directly under the Standing Committee of the Politburo. However, the CCRG took orders from Mao and not from other party leaders.

Mao used the Chinese youth to attack the party-state bureaucrats. High school students and college students formed the Red Guards. The Red Guards took orders from the CCRG. The Red Guards competed among themselves to see who was more loyal to Mao. They demonstrated enormous energy, enthusiasm, and spontaneity. Yet they were manipulated by Mao's CCRG.

On August 8, 1966, a plenum of the CCP Central Committee adopted the "Decision Concerning the Great Proletarian Cultural Revolution." The power struggle was waged by the surprising tactic of mobilizing China's radical younger generation against their elders (and, with the help of the People's Liberation Army (PLA), inducing the latter not to resist). The power-struggle goals would be for the most part achieved by 1968 (with the formal expulsion of Liu Shaoqi and Deng Xiaoping from all their posts and the former from the CCP itself at the 12th Plenum of the 8th CCP Congress in October 1968).

On August 18, 1966, over 1 million Red Guards rallied in Tiananmen Square. Mao also wore the Red Guard armband, and this automatically implied that he had taken on the role of "supreme commander" of the Red Guards. In several more rallies following this meeting, a total of over 10 million Red Guards gathered in Tiananmen Square. They were encouraged by Mao to carry out the Cultural Revolution throughout the country.

Mao used mass movements to destroy the party-state structure influenced by the Liu-Deng line. Mass movements were manipulated by the CCRG to seize power from the existing party-state bureaucrats. However, lacking an organizational structure and well-defined guidelines, the Red Guards began to split into factions.

By the end of 1966, diverse groups of radical workers ("revolutionary rebels"), instigated by the CCRG to incite revolution in the factories, had joined the Red Guards. When different factions of the Red Guards turned against each other and resorted to deadly armed conflict, worker teams were sent in to take over the schools. When workers of different factions were involved in violent conflict, the PLA was sent in to support the "revolutionary left organizations."

In the winter of 1966 and 1967, with the logistic aid of the PLA, the Red Guards and revolutionary rebels managed to undermine the existing party and government apparatus in major cities and provincial capitals. As the party-state structures collapsed and internal fighting broke out between the less-radical and the more-radical groups, Mao had to call on the PLA to intervene. The authority of the military was extended over state and party organs and industrial units. The Revolutionary Committee (RC) was based on a triple alliance among army officers, revolutionary party cadres, and representatives of revolutionary mass organizations. The triple alliances were often dominated by the PLA.

At the 12th Plenary Session of the CCP Congress in October 1968, Liu Shaoqi was officially denounced as a traitor and expelled from the party. On the surface, this was perceived as a political victory for Mao. In the struggle against Liu Shaoqi, the military leader Lin Biao was perceived as Mao's closest ally. The Ninth CCP National Congress in 1969 named Lin as Mao's successor. Forty-five percent of the new Central Committee, whose number had been increased from 190 full and alternative members to 279, was made up of party members with military backgrounds; of the 21-person ruling Politburo, 10 were military commanders. But Mao's suspicions about Lin's personal ambition quickly led to a new round of power struggling. On September 13, 1971, a Chinese air force plane with nine persons aboard crashed 150 miles inside Outer Mongolia. Lin, his wife and son, and a few close associates were killed.

After Lin's demise, the "Gang of Four" emerged as the leader of the radical forces. This left-wing group included Mao's wife Jiang Qing, CCP vice chairman Wang Hongwen, vice premier Zhang Chunqiao, and CCP propaganda chief Yao Wenyuan.

Premier Zhou Enlai led a moderate group that was trying to stabilize the political situation and move China forward on modernization. Zhou's group of moderates included Deng Xiaoping, who was removed from power in 1968 but returned to Beijing in 1973 to become the vice premier. As Zhou's health failed, Deng took on more responsibility and implemented pragmatic policies.

Mao recognized Deng's outstanding ability but did not trust his loyalty to "continuing revolution." Mao abandoned Deng again in early 1976 because of the fear that Deng might reverse the course of the Cultural Revolution. Hua Guofeng, who positioned himself between the leftists and the moderates, received Mao's support in early 1976. In fact, when Zhou Enlai died in January 1976, Mao named Hua Guofeng the acting premier.

Mao Zedong's death on September 9, 1976, brought to an end an era in Chinese history. The Gang of Four was arrested in October 1976. The Cultural Revolution was over. Deng Xiaoping came back to power a year later. Mao once said that he accomplished two major things in his life. One was defeating Chiang Kai-shek and driving him to Taiwan. The other was conducting the Cultural Revolution. The CCP Central Committee resolution in 1981, however, officially declared the Cultural Revolution a disaster. Future historians are not likely to offer a less-strong critique of the Cultural Revolution than the CCP resolution did. As more facts of the brutality of the Cultural Revolution become available, scholars might develop an even harsher assessment of the Cultural Revolution.

The chaos, killing, and, at the end, the stagnation of the Cultural Revolution led Deng Xiaoping to abandon this vain search for a Chinese version of modernity. China had to jump on the bandwagon of successful Western-style modernization that had proved so effective in Taiwan and elsewhere in East Asia. The Cultural Revolution became the economic and social watershed of modern Chinese history.[5] The Cultural Revolution was a terribly costly failure. One hundred million people were adversely affected by the Cultural Revolution. In economic terms, although agricultural production suffered only marginally, there was a drastic decline in industrial production. There was no doubt that China's modernization had suffered a setback. That setback formed a particularly sharp contrast with China's neighbors. It was during the decade of chaos and violence in China's Cultural Revolution that Japan enjoyed an economic miracle. The "four little tigers" (South Korea, Taiwan, Hong Kong, and Singapore) also experienced rapid growth during the decade. The gap between China and advanced countries was not reduced but increased as a result of the Cultural Revolution.

One sector profoundly affected by the Cultural Revolution was education. From 1967 to 1976, China did not have a regular college entrance exam. A generation of students lost the opportunity to pursue college education. It was not until 1977 that Deng Xiaoping decided to allow college entrance exams to admit new students.Deng promoted education and science as critical steps toward China's modernization.

The Cultural Revolution created a legacy of bitterness as well as disillusionment with communism among the young, who had been exploited for political purposes. Mao Zedong's internal policies failed to establish the sociopolitical infrastructure that would have helped realize his vision of national reconstruction.

Mao shared the overriding desire of all 20th-century Chinese revolutionaries to restore China's independence and greatness. Mao's legacy was not altogether negative. In some important ways, he had laid the basis for the developments that, in the post-Mao period, have brought economic growth and international respect to China. The framework for foreign relations established by Mao and Zhou was successful in helping China emerge as a major power by the 1970s.

Mao's investment in heavy industry at the expense of light industry created shortages in consumer goods but laid the foundation for Deng's industrial takeoff. Mao left China practically free of foreign debt, which made the country very attractive to foreign investors. Once the door was opened, foreign investors flooded the Chinese market with funds and manufacturing technology.

Mao's penchant for self-reliance and untrammeled national independence, which had led him, at one stage, to confront both the superpowers concurrently and to develop a nuclear arsenal, had already raised China's global image when Deng took over power.

MAO'S LEGACIES AND THE CAUSES OF REFORM

The failure of the Cultural Revolution led to the end of the revolution era and the beginning of reform and opening. The Cultural Revolution involved serious ideological conflicts and unprecedented mass movements all over the country. The Lin Biao affair discredited the myth that Mao was infallible and deepened the succession crisis. Radicalism went to extreme and was exhausted. The Gang of Four played a radical endgame. The radical upheaval in China and Beijing's radical rhetoric abroad led to extreme diplomatic isolation and escalated Sino-Soviet confrontation. Interestingly, it was during this dangerous time that Mao Zedong initiated (or responded to) a geopolitical transformation of Sino-American relations, with President Richard Nixon's visit to Beijing in 1972. The Sino-American rapprochement had profound implication both for China's internal development (though this might not have been so clear at the beginning) and foreign relations. The Cultural Revolution is a watershed in contemporary Chinese history. The end of this epoch represents the end of the revolution and the beginning of reform.

Mao Zedong left a mixed legacy. As the founder of the PRC and the core leader of the CCP from 1936 to 1976, Mao played the most significant role in the Chinese revolution and in the establishment of the Chinese contemporary political system. Under Mao's leadership, China became a united country. He led an ambitious industrialization effort. From 1949 to 1976, China made great progress in urbanization and modernization. On the other hand, Mao overemphasized the role of "class struggle." He initiated one political campaign after another. Mao often resorted to unconventional political strategy. After the Great Leap Forward and particularly during the Cultural Revolution, Mao carried out reckless policies, persecuted large numbers of party and government officials, manipulated one group of people against another group, and disregarded the party Constitution and law and order. Mao was more adept at revolution than governing.

When Mao passed away in 1976, China was in a deep political crisis. Hua Guofeng had to resort to the extraordinary measure of arresting the "Gang of Four" to settle political differences. Even holding all three top positions of the party, state, and military, Hua was not able to meet the challenge of Deng Xiaoping as soon as Deng came back. By December 1978, Deng successfully pushed Hua aside and became the new paramount leader of China. Although Deng did not claim either the top party or state position, he was recognized as the core leader and final decision maker in the new system. Deng Xiaoping was able to initiate a comprehensive reform and opening policy because of the following factors.

First, after the political turmoil of the Cultural Revolution, the majority of the Chinese elites and the people truly looked for political stability. The revolution was over. It was time for reform and peaceful change. Deng was able to unify the elites and respond to the popular demand for gradual political change.

Second, the Cultural Revolution drove the Chinese economy to the edge of bankruptcy. The profound economic crisis demanded dramatic changes in the economic system. Deng and his supporters were able to make a fundamental shift from Mao's emphasis on class struggle to "taking economic construction as the central task" for the party, the state, and the people. The significance of this decisive and fundamental shift in Chinese politics should not be underestimated.

Third, China was further lagging behind its neighbors, especially the little tigers, including South Korea, Singapore, Hong Kong, and Taiwan. Such sharp contrast pointed out to the Chinese leadership that without economic reform and opening up, China had no future. Interestingly, the little tigers provided valuable lessons for China's reform and opening.

Fourth, reform policies reflected a demand for change from above and popular demand for change from below. Some of the initial reform policies, including the popular and successful household responsibility system in agricultural reform, were not invented by the leadership. To the contrary, the policies simply permitted all famers to do what some peasants had already put into practice in selected areas.

In the next chapter, we will examine China's leaders and their key policies. We will also address the challenging issue of leadership transition.

Chapter 2

China's Leaders and Leadership Transition

MAO ZEDONG AND CONTINUOUS REVOLUTION

Mao Zedong (1893–1976) was the leader of China from the founding of the People's Republic in 1949 until his death in 1976. Mao played the most significant role in the rise of the Chinese Communist Party (CCP) and the success of the Chinese revolution. He participated in the founding conference of the CCP in 1921 and emerged as the core party leader during the Long March in 1935. Mao's influence on Chinese politics was truly profound and long-lasting.[1]

Mao was born to a rich peasant family in the Shaoshan village of Hunan Province in central China. He received several years of traditional Chinese education in his village. In 1910, Mao left the village to study at a school in Xiangtan and then went to Changsha, the capital of Hunan Province, to attend the First Provincial Normal School. At the college, Mao studied both Chinese and Western ideas. He was deeply concerned about China's unfortunate status as a "semifeudal and semicolonial" country. Mao searched hard for new means of national salvation.

In the May Fourth Movement of 1919, Mao was exposed to new ideas about democracy and science. Working as a librarian at Peking University, Mao learned from Professor Li Dazhao, who was a leading intellectual of Marxism, and read books about communism. In 1921 Mao became one of the 12 founders of the CCP. During the First United Front of the CCP and the Nationalist Party (Kuomintang or KMT), Mao was responsible for organizing peasants. China was a predominately peasant country. In 1927 he wrote a report about the peasant movement in Hunan. Mao said:

> The present upsurge of the peasant movement is a colossal event. In a very short time, in China's central, southern, and northern provinces, several hundred million peasants will rise like a mighty storm, like a hurricane, a force so swift and violent that no power, however great, will be able to hold it back. They will smash all the trammels that bind them and rush forward along the road of liberation.[2]

Mao regarded the peasants as the backbone of the Chinese revolution. He believed that whoever could organize and lead the majority of the peasants would be leading Chinese revolution.

After the KMT-CCP split in 1927, Mao led an armed uprising and built a revolutionary base in the Jiangxi Province. The Red Army that Mao and Zhu De led expanded quickly. From 1931 to 1934, the KMT forces launched five encirclement and annihilation campaigns against the Red Army. Growing KMT attacks and internal CCP rivalry resulted in the Red Army's heavy losses in the fifth KMT campaign. As a result, the Communist forces were forced into the legendary Long March. At the Zunyi Conference during the Long March, in January 1935, Mao emerged as a top leader of the CCP. Although the party suffered extreme hardship and heavy losses, the CCP leadership was preserved through the Long March, and the Red Army reached Shaanxi in northwestern China in 1935. The Long March generation, including Mao and Deng Xiaoping, dominated CCP leadership until the beginning of the 1990s.

After the famous Xian incident in December 1936, in which KMT leader Chiang Kai-shek was arrested by his regional commanders Zhang Xueliang and Yang Hucheng, the CCP sent in the skillful leader Zhou Enlai to help negotiate a settlement. Zhou helped to negotiate the release of Chiang in order to unite the country against Japanese invasion. Chiang was released and returned to the capital city of Nanjing, after he promised to stop fighting against the CCP and begin resisting Japanese aggression against China. This was the beginning of the Second United Front between the KMT and the CCP. The united front was instrumental in defeating the Japanese invaders. The Japanese invasion was marked by rampant atrocities to terrorize the population.

The most infamous of these was the "Rape of Nanjing" in late 1937, during which the Chinese estimated that 200,000 to 300,000 were killed and tens of thousands raped.

From 1937 to 1945, the CCP waged guerrilla warfare and established many base areas in the Japanese-occupied regions of China. By the time of Japan's unconditional surrender to the Allied powers, the CCP commanded 1 million troops and 2 million militiamen and controlled 19 "liberated areas" of more than 100 million people. The war of resistance against Japan gave the CCP breathing room from Chiang Kai-shek's obsessive efforts to exterminate it. Mao and the CCP gained broad popular support during the anti-Japanese war.

The Chinese people wanted peace. But the differences between the KMT and the CCP were so profound that it was very difficult for the two sides to reach a consensus. Chiang Kai-shek initially thought that with overwhelming military advantages he could defeat the CCP in a short time. A civil war broke out in 1946. Chiang's forces held huge initial advantages in the quantity of men and material: his forces numbered about 3 million soldiers with 6,000 artillery pieces. The CCP, on the other hand, had armies of about 1 million and just 600 artillery pieces. By 1948, however, the battleground situation turned in favor of the CCP forces. On October 1, 1949, Mao Zedong announced in Beijing that the People's Republic of China (PRC) had been established. The CCP was able to defeat the once more-numerous and better-armed KMT forces because of many reasons. First, the KMT government was corrupt and was not able to maintain order and mitigate inflation in its controlled areas. Second, the CCP was better organized and more disciplined in comparison to its KMT counterparts. Third, the CCP adopted a strategy of surrounding the cities from the countryside. The CCP's land reform policy was very popular among the peasants who formed the majority of China's population. Fourth, Mao advocated a position of "New Democracy" rather than communism. Mao's seemingly democratic approach and effective united front strategy helped the CCP to gain broad support. Finally, after the initial defeat in its early years, the CCP learned the importance of military and was able to build up a disciplined military though the tough battles against KMT and Japanese forces. Mao himself developed into a great military strategist. At the Zunyi Conference in 1935, Mao first gained control of the Red Army, and he soon emerged as the undisputed supreme leader of

Mao Zedong (shown here in a photo published in 1949) was the communist founder of the People's Republic of China. He led China from 1949 to 1976. (The Illustrated London News Picture Library.)

the CCP. Mao was at the helm of the CCP and its Central Military Commission until the end of his life.

A key to Mao's political ascent was the pragmatic ideology and policy that produced revolutionary success. Mao's thought was intensely practical and oriented toward contemporary problems. Mao emphasized "seeking truth from facts" and adopted flexible policies and far-sighted strategies.

In the early years of the PRC, Mao followed the ideas of the New Democracy, which advocated moderate politics, a united front with different political forces, and a mixed economy. However, Mao became increasingly impatient with the relatively slow pace of economic growth and social change. In 1958 he pushed the Great Leap Forward campaign, aimed at "overtaking England and catching up with America" in iron and steel production. He also supported building the people's communes all over the country in a short period of time. The Great Leap Forward unfortunately led to a famine. Taking part of the blame for the failures of the Great Leap policies, Mao retreated to the second front of the leadership by resigning from the presidency of the People's Republic of China.

Mao became increasingly frustrated as a result of his diminished power. In 1962 he again began to emphasize the need for class struggle. Mao developed the theory of "continuous revolution," with class struggle as the key. Under this theory, he launched the Cultural Revolution in 1966. Following Mao's own Bombard the Headquarters wall posters, Chinese youth, organized as Red Guards, traveled about the country at will, generally creating havoc. Beginning in early 1967, government bodies everywhere were gradually displaced in "power seizures" by revolutionary committees, comprised of cadres loyal to Mao, representatives of new mass organizations, and military representatives. The military had to be called in to support Mao's leftists. Chinese president Liu Shaoqi was arrested and soon died in prison. The Cultural Revolution did not officially end until Mao passed away in 1976. The radical political movement created enormous social unrest and brought the Chinese economy to the edge of bankruptcy.

In the early 1970s, Mao dramatically shifted China's foreign policy. After the 1969 clash on the Sino-Soviet border, Mao clearly saw the Soviet Union as the most serious threat to China's national security. Chairman Mao and U.S. president Richard Nixon were able to achieve rapprochement because of their common concerns about the growing Soviet threat. Following U.S. national security adviser Henry Kissinger's pathbreaking visit to Beijing in 1971, President Nixon visited China in February 1972. Mao was able to significantly improve relations not only with the United States but also with many other countries.

As a key leader of the CCP and the founder of the PRC, Mao had a great impact on the Chinese political system. Mao played the most critical role in the CCP resistance against Japan and in the CCP victory over the Nationalist party. Mao's leadership skills and influence grew out of many years of difficult struggle. He achieved great success in the early years of the PRC. After the antirightist campaign in 1957, however, Mao lost his pragmatism and became more concerned with a "continuous revolution" against class enemies. The 1958 Great Leap Forward and the 1966–1976 Cultural Revolution were disasters that seriously interrupted China's modernization.

Mao's legacy will continue to affect China for generations to come. When Deng Xiaoping came back to power in 1977, he urged the CCP to uphold Maoist thought. Deng insisted, however, that the essence of Mao's thought was to "seek truth from fact." In other words, Mao's teaching should not be dogma that would bind the current leadership's thinking and policies. Deng totally rejected both the means and the ends of the Cultural Revolution. Mao's cultural revolution is dead. Indeed, Deng's pragmatic policy of reform and opening has replaced Mao's continuous revolution as the main policy line of the Chinese leadership since 1978.

DENG XIAOPING AND PRAGMATIC REFORM

Deng Xiaoping (1904–1997) was the "core" or "paramount" leader of the second-generation CCP/PRC leadership. Interestingly, Deng never claimed the official top party position (chairman) or the presidency of the PRC. Deng became the "core" leader based on a decision made at a CCP Central Committee plenum in December 1978.

Deng was born to a landlord family in Guangan, Sichuan. At the age of 16 he went to France, where he worked and studied for six years, and then he spent a year in Moscow. Deng joined the Communist Party when he was in France and formed a close friendship with Zhou Enlai. Zhou was one of the most prominent CCP leaders and became premier of China in 1949, staying in that position until his death in 1976. During the early civil war years, Deng became a political commissar in the Red Army. He participated in the legendary Long March. In the anti-Japanese war, Deng served as political commissar of Liu Bocheng's 129th Division, one of the three major components of the Eighth Route Army. In the Huai-Hai campaign of 1948–1949, Deng served as party secretary of the general front committee, which was formed to coordinate the strategy of participating CCP armies. The Huai-Hai campaign was one of the most decisive battles in the CCP-KMT civil war. After the civil war had been won, Deng became the top CCP official in southwest China.

By 1956, Deng became a member of the Politburo Standing Committee, the top decision-making body in the CCP. Deng also served as secretary-general of the CCP from 1956 to 1966. In the Cultural Revolution, Deng was labeled the as the number two CCP person in authority taking the "capitalist road." Both Deng and "number one capitalist roader" Liu Shaoqi, president of the PRC, were pushed out of power in 1966.

In 1973, after the downfall of Lin Biao in 1971, Deng was brought back to Beijing by Mao Zedong to be in charge of key political, economic, and military decision making. Deng took measures to adjust the radical policy of the Cultural Revolution. Deng also engaged in intense struggles against the radical elements of the Cultural Revolution led by Mao's wife, Jiang Qing. Premier Zhou Enlai died in January 1976, and Mao Zedong named Hua Guofeng as acting premier. The mourning of Zhou later turned into a mass protest against radical policies and in support of Deng Xiaoping. On April 5, 1976, the protest in Tiananmen Square was suppressed. Mao was concerned that Deng might reverse the course of the Cultural Revolution, so he removed Deng from power again in April 1976.

In 1977 Deng came back to power, and by December 1978 he had emerged as the core leader in China. Deng played the most significant role in moving China away from Mao's class struggles. Deng's bold policy of reform and opening moved China into an era of rapid growth and comprehensive modernization.

Deng summarized the political guidelines of his leadership as "one focus, two points": the focus was economic construction, and the two points were "reform and opening." He also specified four "cardinal principles." The four cardinal principles were socialism, people's democratic dictatorship, CCP leadership, and Marxism/Maoist thought. Deng consistently emphasized "development, reform, and stability" and insisted that development was the "highest principle."

As Deng's supporters, Hu Yaobang emerged as the general secretary of the CCP, and Zhao Ziyang became the premier of the PRC in 1980. Both Hu and Zhao played significant roles in China's reform and opening. They were once considered likely successors of Deng.

Deng Xiaoping (shown here in a photo published in 1978) was the designer of China's policy of reform and opening. (AP Photo.)

In 1987, however, CCP general secretary Hu Yaobang was removed from power, because Deng and other senior leaders perceived Hu as soft on students who demanded more freedom and democracy. Former premier Zhao Ziyang became the new general secretary, and Li Peng became the new premier. On April 15, 1989, Hu Yaobang passed away after a heart attack. Hundreds of thousands of college students went to Tiananmen Square to pay their respects. Quickly, the student movement gained momentum as an anticorruption and prodemocracy movement. The CCP leadership was divided about how to deal with the student protests. Deng Xiaoping and Li Peng were suspicious of the motives of the protesters and took a hard line against the students. Zhao Ziyang was more sympathetic to the students. With the party leaders unable to resolve their differences, Li Peng declared martial law in Beijing, and Zhao Ziyang was removed from power. Shanghai party secretary Jiang Zemin was selected by Deng Xiaoping and other senior leaders to replace Zhao as the new general secretary. On June 4, 1989, the military was ordered to clear the students from Tiananmen

Square. On June 9, 1989, Deng Xiaoping publicly praised the People's Liberation Army soldiers for restoring order. Deng also told the "third generation" leaders, with Jiang Zemin as the core, that they must continue to carry out reform and opening.

From 1989 to 1991, conservative political forces gained more influence in China. Many reform efforts suffered setbacks. During this same time period, all the former communist regimes in Eastern and Central Europe collapsed. By December 1991, the Soviet Union itself had disintegrated. Deng drew the right lessons from the demise of the Soviet Union and put economic construction before ideology. In 1992, Deng made his famous southern tour to promote market reform and greater opening. During the trip, Deng openly called for speeding up market reform, saying that reform was the only way to move forward and that those who did not support reform should quit. Growth and foreign investment surged. At the CCP National Congress held in October 1992, the party formally committed itself to building a "socialist market economy." China entered a new phase of reform and opening. Deng Xiaoping served as the architect of China's reform.

JIANG ZEMIN AND TECHNOCRATIC POLITICS

Jiang Zemin was born on August 17, 1926, in the city Yangzhou in Jiangsu Province. He studied at the prestigious Shanghai Jiaotong University, where he majored in electrical engineering, and graduated in 1947. During his college years, Jiang participated in the student movement, and he joined the CCP in 1946. In 1955, Jiang traveled to the Soviet Union, where he ended up working as a trainee in the Stalin Automobile Works for a year. After returning to China in 1956, Jiang worked as an engineer and then factory director in Changchun, Wuhan, and Shanghai. He accumulated much management experience through his service for the Ministry of Electronics Industry. In 1985, Jiang was appointed the mayor of Shanghai. During the early 1989 Tiananmen demonstrations, Jiang was able to maintain peace in Shanghai. He took forceful measures to remove a prostudent editor from an influential Shanghai newspaper. He was summoned to the central government to face greater challenges in May 1989.

As the core of the Chinese third-generation leaders, Jiang Zemin upheld and developed Deng Xiaoping's reform and opening policy.

President Jiang Zemin delivers his New Year's address in Beijing on December 31, 2001. (AP Photo/Xinhua, Lan Hongguang.)

Jiang became the general secretary of the CCP and chairman of the Central Military Commission in 1989. In 1993, Jiang was elected president of China by the National People's Congress.

Jiang was keen on modernizing the Chinese economy. At the 15th CCP Congress in 1997, he unveiled a sweeping plan to reform China's state-owned enterprise. In order to further integrate China into the global economy, Jiang strongly promoted Chinese membership in the World Trade Organization (WTO). After many years of tough negotiation,

China finally joined the WTO in December 2001. This move has had a profound and long-lasting impact on China's development as a world power.

Maintaining stability, staying the course begun by Deng Xiaoping, and achieving fast economic growth are among the major achievements of Jiang Zemin. In 2002, Jiang stepped down as general secretary of the CCP, but he remained the chairman of the Central Military Commission. In March 2003, Hu Jintao was elected to become the new president of China. Jiang retired from being chairman of the Central Military Commission in September 2004.

Jiang advocated the "three represents," which stressed that the party should represent (1) the development trend of the advanced productive forces; (2) the orientation of China's advanced culture; and (3) the fundamental interests of the overwhelming majority of the people.[3] Science and technology are the strongest of the productive forces and represent a hallmark of advanced productive forces today. The CCP even accepted members from among entrepreneurs and private property owners. Representing the fundamental interests of the majority of the people helped to broaden the party's basis. However, there has been criticism that Jiang took better care of the intellectual and entrepreneurial classes than of the workers and farmers. During the Jiang era, the gap between rich and poor grew rapidly. Regional disparities also increased significantly.

In the eras of Mao Zedong and Deng Xiaoping, leaders who participated in the long revolution—especially those who joined the legendary Long March of 1934–1935—dominated the top leadership. In the reform era, more and more senior leaders came from a technocratic background. Indeed, this period was a time of "technocratic takeover" within China's party-state leadership. In 1982, professional revolutionaries with university-level technical education constituted just 2 percent of the CCP Central Committee, but by 1987 they made up a quarter of the Central Committee. By 1997 they made up over half. All of the nine members of the Politburo Standing Committee elected in 2002 were engineers, including the three top leaders: General Secretary Jiang Zemin (electrical engineer), National People's Congress chairman Li Peng (civil engineer), and Premier Zhu Rongji (electrical engineer). This is also true of the current leadership's top three: General Secretary Hu Jintao (hydraulic engineer), National People's Congress chairman

Wu Bangguo (electrical engineer), and Premier Wen Jiabao (geological engineer).[4] Their technical background and political loyalty served the CCP's new mission of modernization under the party leadership. Lacking the revolutionary credential, the new source of legitimacy became economic development. It was in the Jiang era that China formally declared the goal of building a "socialist market economy" and establishing a system based on the rule of law. China joined the World Trade Organization in 2001. That accomplishment was a milestone in China's move toward a market economy.

While China's economy was rapidly moving forward after 1992, political reforms lagged behind. Rampant corruption developed all over the country. Many rounds of anticorruption campaigns failed to stop official corruption. A root cause of corruption is the lack of effective checks of power. The weak legal system also allowed people with powerful connections to exploit opportunities in the chaotic socioeconomic transition. The rise of corruption and lack of social justice have become key sources of social instability.[5]

Jiang's leadership can be seen as ushering in the era of relatively consensual elite politics in China after the volatile strongman rule of Mao and Deng. On the foreign policy front, Jiang Zemin improved relations with the great powers and also expanded China's global reach. The Chinese economy achieved rapid growth; socioeconomic inequality also expanded quickly. The coastal regions grew most rapidly, but inland areas did not grow at comparable pace. Jiang has a mixed legacy. In comparison with the dramatic changes under Mao and Deng, the Jiang era seemed relatively calm. Perhaps maintaining political stability during a period of rapid and profound socioeconomic transition itself is a remarkable achievement. Future generations might give the Jiang leadership more credit for moving China toward the market economy.

HU JINTAO AND THE HARMONIOUS SOCIETY

Hu Jintao was born into a family of educators in December 1942 in Anhui Province. He became a student leader at the prestigious Tsinghua University in the 1960s. Soon after graduating, Hu went to work at the grassroots in Gansu Province in 1968. Gansu is one of the least developed provinces of China. Working in Gansu for over a decade helped Hu to obtain a deep sense of China's diversity and regional inequality.

In 1992, Hu was promoted to join the secretariat of the Chinese Communist Youth League (CCYL) and become president of the All-China Youth Federation in Beijing.[6] Thanks to CCP general secretary Hu Yaobang's patronage, Hu Jintao became first secretary of the CCYL in 1984. He had assumed a ministerial-level position at the age of 42—one of the youngest ministerial-level cadres in the post–Cultural Revolution era. Hu developed extensive ties with other leaders in the CCYL. Leaders with background in the CCYL now form a powerful group in the Chinese party and state leadership.

From 1985 to 1988, Hu served as the top party leader in Guizhou Province, which is one of the poorest areas of China. From 1988 to 1992, he was the CCP secretary in Tibet. Hu demonstrated his political skills and toughness during this period. Hu had some populist and promarket inclinations. Yet at critical moments when the CCP was threatened, he was bold and resolute in crushing the party's enemies.[7] Hu was moved from Lhasa to Beijing in 1992 to become a member of the powerful Politburo Standing Committee of the CCP Central Committee. It was widely believed that Deng Xiaoping promoted Hu Jintao to the Standing Committee of the CCP Politburo, opening the door for him to succeed Jiang Zemin as the "core" of the Communist Party's fourth generation of leaders. Hu took up key tasks of handling personnel matters. He also served as president of the Central Party School, which is in charge of training high-level party officials.

In the decade between 1992 and 2002, Hu worked diligently but maintained a low profile. He became vice president of the PRC in 1998. At the CCP 16th National Congress in 2002, Hu succeeded Jiang Zemin as the general secretary of the CCP Central Committee. The power transition was remarkably smooth, considering the party's long history of difficult leadership transition. The leadership transition was completed when Hu succeeded Jiang as chairman of the CCP Central Military Commission in 2004. Although Jiang stepped down from all of his official positions, he retains strong political influence as the former top party leader.

Recognizing the widening gap between the rich and poor and growing regional disparities, Hu has called for building a "harmonious society." This is an effort aimed at addressing the challenges raised through overemphasis on gross domestic product (GDP) growth by paying more attention to social problems and social justice. Premier Wen

Hu Jintao, president of China (2003–). (Department of Defense.)

Jiabao also came from a humble background. Like Hu, Wen worked in the less-developed province of Gansu for many years before he was transferred to Beijing. They both have detailed knowledge about the common people and the dramatic regional disparities existing in China.

Another ideological innovation of Hu Jintao is the "scientific view of economic and social development." One important aspect of Hu's "scientific development" is that economic progress should not merely enrich one sector of the population or one region of the country. The scientific development must take into consideration the welfare of the entire country as well as the fundamental and long-term interests of the people. Another important aspect of scientific development is harmony among production, the environment, and quality of life. The past single-minded emphasis on GDP growth has meant that China has entered into a vicious cycle of more production, more pollution.

The Hu-Wen leadership has paid more attention to education, public health, and the environment. However, critics point out that there has been a lot of talk but not enough action.

LEADERSHIP TRANSITION AND CHINA'S FUTURE

Leadership transition has often been difficult in Chinese politics. Mao Zedong remained the top leader of the CCP and the PRC until his death in 1976. Several arranged succession plans failed. The transition from Jiang Zemin to Hu Jintao, in contrast, was remarkably smooth. It remains to be seen whether the 2012 leadership transition from Hu to a new generation will come free of surprises.

Although it is difficult to predict the future by just looking at the past, it is useful to have an overview of China's past leadership transitions. In the early 1960s, Liu Shaoqi was number two in the CCP leadership and was the president of the PRC. It was widely believed that he would be Mao's successor. However, serious policy differences developed between Mao and Liu. In 1966, Mao initiated the radical Cultural Revolution in order to oust Liu and his close associate Deng Xiaoping, who was secretary-general of the CCP at that time. Both Liu and Deng were pushed out of power. Liu died in prison in 1969. Deng was sent down to work in a machine factory as a mechanic.

After the downfall of Liu Shaoqi, Minister of Defense Lin Biao emerged as Mao's "closest comrade in arms" and vice chairman of the CCP. The Ninth National Congress of the CCP in 1969 officially designated Lin Biao as Mao's successor. Ironically, Lin's successor status was written into the CCP Constitution. But serious differences soon emerged between Mao and Lin. After a failed assassination attempt against Mao, Lin Biao and his wife and son tried to fly to the Soviet Union. They died in an airplane crash in Mongolia on September 13, 1971. The Lin Biao incident seriously discredited the once popular notion that Mao was always right. Many people in China began to question Mao's judgment. Some started to examine the problems of the political system.

Frustrated by the two failed attempts, Mao began to search for new successors. He considered the Shanghai rebel leader Wang Hongwen, because Wang had the experience of being a farmer, soldier, and industrial worker. Wang was quickly promoted from city leadership in

Shanghai to become a vice chairman of the CCP. However, Mao quickly discovered that Wang did not have the necessary political wisdom and skills to lead China.

In 1973, Mao called Deng Xiaoping back to Beijing and put him in charge of the daily running of the government, as Premier Zhou Enlai's health was in decline. Deng was an extraordinarily experienced and skillful political leader with deep roots and broad support. He quickly took actions to strengthen discipline in the military and bring the economy back to order. There was no doubt about Deng's ability to govern. However, Mao Zedong became increasingly concerned that Deng might reverse the radical course of the Cultural Revolution. As a result, Mao was not willing to pass the leadership to Deng. When Premier Zhou Enlai passed away in January 1976, Mao Zedong named relatively unknown Hua Guofeng as the acting premier. Deng Xiaoping was once again removed from power when Mao lost trust in him. Hua Guofeng was elevated by Mao to the positions of first vice chairman of the CCP Central Committee and premier.

Mao Zedong died on September 9, 1976. There was an intense power struggle between Premier Hua Guofeng and the Gang of Four—Politburo members Jiang Qing (Mao's wife), Zhang Chunqiao (vice premier), Wang Hongwen (CCP vice chairman), and Yao Wenyuan (propaganda chief). On October 6, 1976, a group of anti–Gang of Four leaders, with Hua Guofeng and Marshal Ye Jianying at its core, arrested Jiang Qing and her followers. Hua assumed the top party, state, and military positions shortly after the death of Mao.

Hua Guofeng was simultaneously chairman of the CCP Central Committee, chairman of the Central Military Commission, and premier of the State Council. Holding the top positions in the party, military, and state, Hua's power and authority seemed to be unmatched by anyone else in China at that time. It was widely circulated that Mao once wrote to Hua that "with you in charge, my heart is at ease." In the official media, Hua was called the "wise leader," and a cult of personality was developing about him. In reality, however, the right to govern cannot simply be given by one leader to another. Real power and authority must be earned. In the case of Hua, his power base was relatively weak. Hua turned out to be a transitional figure in Chinese politics.

In 1977, Deng Xiaoping returned to power as vice chairman of the CCP and vice premier. As Hua was advocating that whatever Mao said and whatever Mao did could not be changed, Deng and his supporters argued that "practice is the sole criterion of truth." After intense policy debates and power struggle, by December 1978 Deng's policy of reform and opening became the official line of the CCP. Soon the top three positions occupied by Hua were taken over by Deng and his close supporters. Hua was replaced by Zhao Ziyang as the premier in 1980 and by Hu Yaobang as the chairman of the CCP in 1981. Deng became the chairman of the Central Military Commission in 1981.

Although Deng Xiaoping only held the title of chairman of the Central Military Commission, he was the de facto top leader of China. In 1982 the position of CCP chairman was abolished. Hu Yaobang was elected to the newly created position of general secretary of the CCP. Hu was considered the successor of Deng. After a series of student movements in 1986, Hu was forced to resign in 1987 from his post as general secretary. The hard-liners believed that the student protests were a consequence of Hu's tolerance of China's liberal intellects, who were pushing for more political freedom and reform.

Zhao Ziyang was named the general secretary of the CCP Central Committee in 1987. Li Peng succeeded Zhao as the premier. As an open-minded reformer, Zhao continued to push forward economic reform and explored the possibility of political reform. Chinese society was facing an uncertain future as the economy encountered high inflation in 1989. The death of former CCP general secretary Hu Yaobang caused student demonstrations in Tiananmen in April 1989. On the critical issue of how to handle the student protests, serious differences developed between Zhao Ziyang and his supporters, on the one hand, and Deng Xiaoping and his supporters, including Premier Li Peng. While Zhao was leaning toward more tolerance, Deng was in favor of ending the protests with whatever means were necessary. Deng strongly believed that stability should prevail. Deng and other senior leaders had a deep fear of political chaos, partially out of the disastrous consequences of the turmoil of the Cultural Revolution. Deng decided to impose martial law and use force to bring the protests to an end. Zhao Ziyang was pushed out of power in May 1989. On June 4, 1989, martial law was enforced through a military crackdown on the student protesters.

Jiang Zemin emerged as the "core of the third generation" of CCP leaders, serving as general secretary of the CCP from 1989 to 2002, as president of the PRC from 1993 to 2003, and as chairman of the Central Military Commission from 1989 to 2004. Unlike Hu Yao-bang and Zhao Ziyang, who did not have an opportunity to lead the military, Jiang became the chairman of the Central Military Commission with strong support from Deng Xiaoping. When Deng resigned from the chairmanship of the Central Military Commission, he said that "Comrade Jiang Zemin is well qualified to be Chairman of the Military Commission because he is well qualified to be General Secretary of the Party."[8] The transition from Deng to Jiang took place gradually, because even after Deng retired, he continued to exercise enormous influence over party policy. The best example was Deng's southern tour in 1992, which fundamentally changed the course of China's reform by speeding up the market-oriented reform and comprehensive opening policy.

As Deng's health declined quickly after 1993, Jiang consolidated his position as the core third-generation leader. When Deng Xiaoping died in 1997, Jiang gave the eulogy at the state funeral and publicly declared that China would continue to move on the path of reform and opening. In the era of reform and opening, Deng's theory effectively replaced Maoist thought as the guiding principles for the Chinese leadership.

At the 1992 CCP National Congress, Hu Jintao was promoted to be a Politburo Standing Committee member. As the youngest member in the Standing Committee, Hu naturally became a future successor to Jiang Zemin. The transition of power from Jiang to Hu was remarkably smooth and came with no big surprises. Hu replaced Jiang as the general secretary of the CCP in 2002, as president of the PRC in 2003, and finally as chairman of the Central Military Commission in 2004. Interestingly, Hu has not been described as the "core" of the fourth-generation leaders. It seems that there is much more emphasis on collective leadership rather than emphasis on a particular individual leader.

In the current Politburo Standing Committee, elected in the CCP 17th National Congress in 2007, Hu Jintao is the first among equals. Wu Bangguo is the chairman of the National People's Congress, and Wen Jiabao is the premier. The two youngest members are Xi Jinping (born in 1953) and Li Keqiang (born in 1955). In 2012, the CCP 18th National Congress will elect the next generation of leaders. Among the current Politburo Standing Committee members, Xi Jinping and Li

Chinese deputy premier Li Keqiang waves to the press before meeting Spain's King Juan Carlos at the Zarzuela Palace on the outskirts of Madrid January 5, 2011. (AP Photo/Paul White.)

Keqiang are most likely to remain and become core members of the next leadership.

As China becomes more modern and democratic, it is most likely that China's future leadership transitions will be more transparent and more institutionalized. Over the long run, democratic election is the only way to provide credible legitimacy to the leadership. It is not an issue of if, but when, China will have popular elections of its national leaders. Part of the argument against direct election of national leaders is that the people are not well educated. In fact, many countries began their democratic elections at or below the level of China's educational development today.

In an ideal situation, it will take a joint reform effort from above and a popular movement from below to realize China's democratic transition. Political leadership is critical for the success of such a transition. Nonelected leaders who have vested interests in the current system might resist movement to a more open and transparent system of leadership transition. Over the long run, however, there may be no viable alternative but to hold popular elections for key national positions.

In the current political system, the CCP controls all key positions. From the offices of president, premier, and cabinet members to those of governors, general managers of large state-owned enterprises, and presidents of key universities, none of those important positions can be filled without prior approval of the CCP. The CCP is becoming more elitist and more professional. Today's leaders are better educated than their predecessors. Although the majority of leaders still have a technical background, a growing number of leaders are trained in law, economics, and public administration.

Leadership struggle is no longer as brutal as it used to be. In the past, the losers of political struggle could lose everything, including their own lives. In today's politics, the ones who lose power might still lead a normal life. The development of the market economy has created a growing nonstate sector. In fact, many former officials have jumped into the sea of business. The growth of private business and foreign investment, along with the rise of a middle class, are affecting Chinese politics. If the current trend of rapid socioeconomic development and political institutionalization continues, China's future development will be more open, prosperous, and sustainable. Leadership transition is a critical factor in this development.

Chapter 3

The CCP as a Governing Party

FROM REVOLUTIONARY PARTY TO GOVERNING PARTY

The Chinese Communist Party (CCP) was founded in 1921. From 1921 to 1949, the CCP was a revolutionary party that engaged in revolutionary movements aimed at overthrowing the old regimes. After defeating the Kuomintang (Nationalist Party) in a civil war from 1946 to 1949, the CCP became a ruling party when the People's Republic of China (PRC) was established in October 1949. Under Mao Zedong, the key themes were class struggle and "continuous revolution." In many ways the CCP continued to behave like a revolutionary party until the mid-1970s.

Deng Xiaoping's reform and opening policy represented a paradigm shift from Mao's class struggle. Deng brought fundamental changes to the thinking and behavior of the CCP leadership. Deng's reform was a peaceful revolution that resulted in the CCP's transformation from being a revolutionary party to a governing party in a modernizing society. China has entered the transition from being a developing country to a newly industrialized one. As a result, the CCP faces new challenges in building good governance and providing public goods.[1]

Deng's successor, Jiang Zemin, fully realized that the CCP should no longer behave like a revolutionary party. Jiang's "three represents" reflected the desire of the party to change with the times. As a governing party in a modernizing China, the CCP is no longer just the "vanguard" of the proletariat. The party is trying to represent the advanced productive forces, the advanced culture, and the fundamental interest of the overwhelming majority of the people. Such new orientation has had significant impact on the development of the CCP as a governing party.

Hu Jintao's "harmonious society" and "scientific development" outlook represent another major development of the CCP as a governing party. As a result of the earlier reforms, China has achieved rapid economic growth but also experienced the growing gap between the rich and poor and between the coastal regions and the heartland. There are growing tensions in society. Harmonious society is designed to reduce such tensions and build sustainable governance. At the same time, a growing number of Chinese scholars and policy makers realize that China's current pattern of economic growth is not sustainable, due to its heavy reliance on energy and raw material consumption. The scientific development outlook is an effort in search of new patterns of growth that will reduce damages to the environment. This new path emphasizes the development of education, human capital, and new technology.

What are the main features of a revolutionary party? A revolutionary party is devoted to destroying the old regime and creating a new system based on revolutionary ideology. It emphasizes change over stability. It often leads to the emergence of a charismatic leader like Mao Zedong. The party might not be very well institutionalized. It often runs against the tides. It does not hesitate to confront real and/or imagined enemies at home and abroad. The top leaders tend to stay in power until they die or they are pushed out of power by other leaders. Revolutionary success provides legitimacy to the party.

What are the main features of a governing party? In China's case, the task of destroying the old regime had been completed by the revolutionary party. The governing party is more interested in preserving and improving the system rather than destroying the system. By nature, a governing party tends to favor reform over revolution. It tends to favor stability over change. But sometimes the best way to preserve stability is through change. A governing party requires a collective leadership rather than a charismatic leader. The party is more institutionalized. There are term limits for key leadership positions and well-established mechanisms for power transition. The party has to earn its legitimacy by promoting economic development, enhancing people's living standards, and maintaining social stability. In an interview with CNN, Premier Wen Jiabao discussed this point:

> My view is that a political party after it becomes a ruling party should be somewhat different from the one when it was struggling for power. The biggest difference should be that this political party should act in accordance with the constitution and the law. The policies and propositions of a political party can be translated into parts of the constitution and the laws through appropriate legal procedures. All political parties, organizations, and all people should abide by the constitution and laws without any exception. They must all act in accordance with the constitution and laws. I see that as a defining feature of modern political system development.[2]

Is it reasonable to argue that the governing party has taken root in China? The era of revolution is over. The main task is modernization. China needs a governing party rather than a revolutionary party. The CCP has transitioned to a governing party. Recent history has indicated that the CCP is a well-established ruling party. With the decline of revolutionary fever and ideology, the CCP must continuously demonstrate its ability to govern by providing tangible results in economic and social policy arenas. The CCP is likely to enjoy popular support as long as the Chinese economy is growing at reasonably rapid pace, the society is basically stable, and China's relations with neighboring countries and major world powers are well managed. The party may encounter crisis if there are serious difficulties in sustaining economic growth and maintaining social stability. International crisis might play a role, but is not likely to undermine the rule of the CCP.

As a governing party with a near monopoly of power in China, the CCP has enormous responsibility for managing China's domestic development and foreign relations. General Secretary Hu Jintao has said that the party should have compassion for the people and use its power for the people. Hu's likely successor, Xi Jinping, has said that power comes from the people. The CCP can be developed into a truly modern and popular political party if its leaders sincerely believe that all political power comes from the people and should be used for the people. There is a huge gap between theory and practice in today's China on the relationship between the CCP and the people. This point is clearly demonstrated in the relationship between the CCP and the National People's Congress (NPC). According the Chinese Constitution, the NPC is the highest organ of power. In reality, however, NPC leader candidates are selected by the CCP leadership. For most key state leadership positions, there is only one candidate for one position. In fact, both the selections of the NPC delegates and the elections in the NPC are strongly influenced by the CCP. Candidates for the most important state positions are selected by the CCP Central Committee. In most cases, the NPC delegates simply vote to approve the slate of candidates provided by the CCP. The ultimate source of political power in China is the CCP. It is impossible to understand contemporary Chinese politics without learning the key CCP institutions.

KEY PARTY INSTITUTIONS

The National Congress of the CCP is the most important political convention in China. The National Party Congress convenes for about two weeks once every five years. The last party congress met in October 2007 and had 2,213 delegates. The next National Congress of the CCP is scheduled to take place in 2012.

The party congress elects the Central Committee and the Central Commission for Discipline Inspection. The current Central Committee has 371 members, including 204 full members and 167 alternates. The Central Commission for Discipline Inspection has 127 members. In theory, the Central Committee elects the Politburo (25 members), the Politburo Standing Committee (9 members), the general secretary of the CCP, and the Central Military Commission (12 members). In practice, however, the process is top down rather than bottom up: members of these leading organs of the CCP dictate the selection of members to the lower-level leadership bodies, such as the Central Committee, which then "approve" the slate of candidates for higher-level positions, such as the next Politburo and its Standing Committee.[3]

The Central Committee convenes at least once per year, in meetings called plenary sessions. Since the 1982 National Congress of the CCP, the party has followed the method of "more candidates than available seats" for the election of the Central Committee. So far, there have

Xinhuamen (Gate of New China), the entrance to Zhongnanhai—the compound that houses the leadership of both the Chinese Communist Party and the State Council. (Photograph taken by Guoli Liu.)

been only a few more candidates than available seats. The CCP leaders intend to increase the number of candidates in the future, in order to make the elections more competitive and more meaningful. It is possible that the CCP might also increase the candidates for the selection of the Politburo in the future. The inner-party elections are important components of the CCP's reform strategy to gradually make China's party system more open and competitive, without weakening its "leading role."[4] At the 5th Plenary of the 17th Central Committee, held in October 2010, Vice President Xi Jinping was appointed the vice chairman of the Central Military Commission. This was widely perceived as a clear indication that Xi might succeed Hu Jintao as the top CCP leader at the 18th National Congress of the CCP in 2012.

The Politburo and its Standing Committee are the most important decision-making organs in the CCP. Of the 25 members of the current Politburo, 7 primarily represent CCP organizations, 10 come from government organizations, 2 come from the military, and 6 come from provincial-level administrative units. The truly powerful inner circle is the Standing Committee of the Politburo.

The current Standing Committee includes the following nine members (based on their official ranking in the committee): Hu Jintao, CCP general secretary, PRC president, and chairman of the Central Military Commission; Wu Bangguo, chairman of the NPC; Wen Jiabao, premier; Jia Qinglin, chairman of the Chinese People's Political Consultative Conference; Li Changchun, secretary of the Central Committee of Ethical and Cultural Construction; Xi Jinping, PRC vice president and executive member of the Secretariat; Li Keqiang, executive vice premier; He Guoqiang, secretary of the Central Commission for Discipline Inspection; and Zhou Yongkang, secretary of the Central Commission of Politics and Law. Indeed, the Politburo Standing Committee members are the top party-state leaders of China. The two youngest members, Xi Jinping (born in 1953) and Li Keqiang (born in 1955), are most likely to be the leading members of the next Politburo Standing Committee to be elected at the 2012 National Congress of the CCP.

China's Vice President Xi Jinping speaks at a press conference at the presidential house in Kingston, Jamaica, February 12, 2009. (AP Photo/Collin Reid.)

The Central Commission for Discipline Inspection plays a crucial role in monitoring and punishing abuse of power, corruption, and other wrongdoings committed by party officials. Lower-level party organizations, including provincial, municipal, and county-level bodies, also have discipline inspection commissions that report directly to the commission one level above them.[5] The discipline inspection commissions play a critical role in Chinese politics, since the system lacks separation of power and a functioning checks and balances system. No major official is likely to be charged by the judicial system until he or she is investigated by the discipline inspection commission.

The Secretariat is an important leadership body that handles the CCP's routine business and administrative matters. The current Secretariat has six members, headed by Xi Jinping. Secretariat members meet daily and are responsible for coordinating the country's major events and important meetings, as well as top leaders' foreign and domestic travel. The Secretariat supervises the work of the General Office of the CCP as well as the party's four central departments. The Organization Department determines the personnel appointments of several thousand high-ranking leadership positions in the party, government, and military, as well as in large state-owned business firms, key universities, and other institutions. Since 2007, the head of the Organization Department has been Politburo member Li Yuanchao. The Publicity Department is primarily responsible for propaganda and controlling the media. The United Front Work Department deals with issues concerning Taiwan, Hong Kong, and Macao, as well as ethnic and religious issues, such as Tibetan affairs. It also manages the CCP's relations with eight "democratic parties" in China. Those democratic parties all support the leadership of the CCP. The International Liaison Department manages the CCP's relations with foreign political parties.[6]

The central party leadership is divided into small "leading groups," focusing respectively on economics, foreign policy, public security, rural affairs, party building, and propaganda and thought work. Each small leading group will coordinate relevant party organizations and government ministries.

Below the center there are 31 provincial committees, including 22 provinces, 5 ethnic autonomous regions (Tibet, Xinjiang, Ningxia, Guangxi, and Inner Mongolia), and 4 centrally administered municipalities (Beijing, Shanghai, Tianjin, and Chongqing). The party secretary of each province is the top leader in the province. The governor is normally the deputy party secretary and thus the second-ranking official in the province. At one level below, there are 665 city committees. The top official in each city is the party secretary. The mayor is the deputy party secretary. The CCP has 2,487 county committees, 41,636 township committees, and 780,000 village committees.[7] The party is everywhere.

The organizational principle of the CCP is the Leninist concept of democratic centralism. The principle requires that the individual is subordinate to the organization, that low-level organizations are subordinate to higher-level organizations, and that all party organizations are subordinate to the CCP center. In principle, there are bottom-up inner party elections at the party congress. In reality, the candidate selection is often done from top to bottom. For the most important positions, there is only one candidate for one position in the elections. The CCP organization is more centralist than democratic.

CORE FEATURES OF THE PARTY IN TRANSITION

The CCP has almost completed the transition from a revolutionary party to a governing party. The party today is still in transition, as China is undergoing modernization, urbanization, industrialization, and a communication revolution. The changing nature of the CCP reflects the needs of China's great transitions.

The party's leadership is becoming younger, better educated, and more professional, from the basic level all the way to the party center. The majority of the middle- and upper-level cadres are college educated. Some have graduate degrees. For instance, Xi Jinping has a BS in chemical engineering and a PhD in law from Tsinghua University, and Li Keqiang holds a BA in law and a PhD in economics from Peking University. Leadership transition is becoming more institutionalized. Central-local relations continue to evolve, as more officials from Beijing are being appointed to the provinces. On the other hand, the center also recruits provincial officials to serve in the central party and state organs. The CCP often relocates provincial leaders.

The party organization is becoming more modern. The CCP is representing a broader range of interests. It is managing an increasingly complex economy and society. With less ideological restraint and more material attractions, the party officials are confronting unprecedented challenges of corruption and abuse of power. Indeed, it is widely recognized by the CCP leadership that corruption is so rampant that it has become an issue of life and death for the party. The CCP has engaged in numerous campaigns against corruption. Unfortunately, there has been no effective way to prevent corruption problems.

The role of the military is changing. "The Party commands the gun" is becoming a well-established norm. There is no professional military representation in the top leadership body, the Politburo Standing Committee. Hu Jintao, chairman of the Central Military Commission, and Xi Jinping, vice chairman of the Central Military Commission, are both civilian leaders. They obtained the top military positions because of their positions in the CCP. There are only 2 generals in the 25-member Politburo. The days when the military was heavily represented in the Politburo, during the Cultural Revolution, are long gone and are not likely to return in the future.

The CCP has a well-developed "Party School" system. All cadres are regularly trained in the party schools, focusing on party ideology, policy studies, management skills, and scientific and technological knowledge. The Central Party School in Beijing is mostly responsible for training high-level officials. In recent years, it also offers training to county and city party secretaries. For participants, attending the Central Party School has a number of advantages. First, it is a mark of honor within the party to be singled out. Second, it gives local officials a privileged inside view of current senior party thinking that will enable them to better second-guess situations once they return to their locality. Third, it provides an ideal source for networking among up-and-coming leaders.[8]

The CCP is becoming more elitist. Most of the Central Committee members are high-level party and government officials. Even among the delegates to the National Congress, there are only a small number who come directly from the ranks of workers and farmers. In recent years, the CCP actively recruits members from colleges, research institutes, the military, and business groups. As Chinese society becomes more open and prosperous, the party is trying to represent a broader range of interests.

In external relations, the CCP's International Liaison Department traditionally focused on managing relations with other communist parties. With the collapse of the Soviet Union and decline of the communist parties in Central and Eastern European countries, the CCP has gradually shifted from its focus on communist parties to developing ties with all major political parties in the world. The CCP has been paying close attention to why some long-established ruling parties would suddenly lose power. The demise of the Soviet Communist Party caused alarm among the CCP leaders. Deng Xiaoping and other Chinese reformers' reaction to the Soviet collapse was to deepen socioeconomic reforms.

The CCP no longer enjoys the strong discipline and deep commitment among its members that typified its earlier years. Nevertheless, the CCP continues to play the dominant role in deciding China's development strategy and key policies. Party decisions determine who will join the elite and what positions they will hold in public bodies. Furthermore, the CCP also decides China's foreign and security policies.[9]

In contrast to the prereform era, the CCP directly manages a smaller share of the economy, due to the dramatic growth of the private sector and foreign investment business in China. Nevertheless, the CCP continues to dominate the state-owned sectors that control vital areas in financial services, energy, communication, transportation, and some other fields. With state tax revenue growing at a double-digit rate in recent years, the CCP is able to guide investment in areas that it considers critical to the mission of modernization and "scientific development." In response to the 2008 global financial crisis, for instance, China decided to invest $600 billion in building infrastructure. Before the 1980s, China had no highway system. By 2010, all counties in China were connected by highways. China is on its way to building the largest highway system in the world. In December 2010, a passenger train in China hit a record speed of 302 miles per hour, the fastest speed ever recorded by a conventional commercial train. The record occurred during a test run of a new track running between Beijing and Shanghai, a rail line that should be open for travel sometime in 2012. The line is expected to reduce the travel time between Beijing and Shanghai by more than half. China's high-speed rail network is expected to expand to 10,000 miles of coverage by 2020. CCP leaders have realized that China's past pattern of extensive growth, meaning growth relying on more input of raw materials and labor, is not sustainable. The party has emphasized shifting to a new pattern of sustainable growth. Chinese leaders have proposed an ambitious goal: to reduce 40–45 percent of energy intensity from its

A man bows down to check a CRH380A high-speed Chinese passenger train outside the venue of the Seventh World Congress on High Speed Rail in Beijing, China, December 7, 2010. The CRH380A is the model that hit a record speed of 302 miles per hour (486 kilometers per hour) during a test run of a yet-to-be-opened link between Beijing and Shanghai. (AP Photo/Alexander F. Yuan.)

2005 level by the year 2020. Energy intensity is a measure of the energy efficiency of a nation's economy. It is calculated as units of energy per unit of gross domestic product (GDP). At the same time, China's total energy consumption has been rising rapidly. Although China is heavily investing in new renewable energy, such as wind power and solar power, it is not willing to cut energy consumption so deeply that it slows down its economic growth. The high economic growth rate has often come at heavy environmental costs.

DENGISM: "SEEK TRUTH FROM FACTS"

The success of the revolution led the CCP into power in 1949. Mao Zedong believed in class struggle and ruled China according to the theory of "continuous revolution." He launched a series of political campaigns, including the Great Leap Forward and the Cultural Revolution. The Cultural Revolution decade, beginning in 1966, seriously destroyed the party's legitimacy and credibility. When Deng Xiaoping came back to power in 1977, he was determined to change course and rebuild the CCP. Debate on the idea that "practice is the sole criterion of truth" prepared the ground for reform and opening.

Deng Xiaoping was a long-time party builder. He began party work in the 1920s, participated in the legendary Long March, and served as a party secretary in the CCP-led military during the anti-Japanese war and the civil wars. At the 1956 National Congress of the CCP, Deng was appointed the general secretary of the Secretariat. He was removed from power when the Cultural Revolution broke out in 1966 and sent to Jiangxi Province to work in a tractor factory. In 1973, Mao called Deng back to Beijing to manage the day-to-day affairs of the party and the state. In April 1976, Deng was removed from power again. With popular support and the backing of senior party leaders, Deng was able to come back to power in 1977. At the 3rd Plenary Session of the 11th CCP Central Committee in December 1978, Deng was able to persuade the party to adopt the new policy of reform and opening.

Except for Mao Zedong, Deng Xiaoping had the most profound impact on the course of the CCP and the PRC's development. Deng was a true modernizer, who pushed China forward. Deng believed that a major factor holding China back was the closed door policy practiced by generations of Chinese leaders. Evidence from the little Asian tigers' economic miracles convinced Deng that China must open its door in order to compete and grow in the era of globalization.

Deng reversed the course of the Cultural Revolution. The violent and chaotic mass campaigns taught a tough lesson to the Chinese leaders: modernization could not be achieved in a lawless and unstable environment. As a victim of the political turmoil and lawless persecution, Deng tried hard to rebuild party and state institutions. He believed that institutionalization was a key to preserving political stability, which was essential for healthy socioeconomic development. As part of efforts to reinvigorate the ranks of the CCP, between 1982 and 1992 Deng set up the Central Advisory Commission, an organization to ease elderly senior leaders into retirement. The CCP has successfully resolved the issue of retirement of senior leaders by instating term limits and age limits. Deng also launched a program for fast-tracking promising young cadres who had college educations and good administrative skills.

Deng Xiaoping believed that China's reform could not succeed without the leadership of the CCP. In 1979, Deng emphasized that modernization was the party's main task. He also laid out the "four cardinal principles" that were "the basic prerequisite for achieving modernization":

1. We must keep to the socialist road.
2. We must uphold the dictatorship of the proletariat.
3. We must uphold the leadership of the Communist Party.
4. We must uphold Marxism-Leninism and Mao Zedong Thought.[10]

Fundamentally speaking, Deng's principles all boil down to the principle of upholding the leadership of the CCP.

Two outstanding characteristics of China are that it is a populous country and it is a developing country. Such characteristics demand that China put economic construction as a top priority. Deng rationalized the "socialist market economy" by saying that China is in the "primary," or "initial," stage of socialism. Deng repeatedly urged Chinese leaders to stop ideological debate over the market in order to focus on developing the economy. After 1989, Deng emphasized economic development as a "hard" principle, meaning that the party had to devote itself to rapid economic development in order to survive and prosper. To promote economic development, the party leadership has given priority to expanding China's education and recruiting college graduates into the party. Such moves not only work in favor of economic development, but they also are helpful for the party. It is interesting that it took a leader with Deng's strong revolutionary credentials to move the CCP away from its revolution mode and into the role of a governing party. Deng's transformative leadership has enabled the CCP to move from a revolutionary party toward a governing party focused on building a modern China.

JIANG ZEMIN: "THREE REPRESENTS"

As a successor to Deng, Jiang Zemin tried to follow Deng's path of reform and opening. Jiang's ideological innovation is called the "three represents," which he first expressed during an inspection tour of Guangdong Province in 2000:

1. The party should represent the advanced productive forces in society.
2. The party should represent advanced modern culture.
3. The party should represent the interests of the vast majority of the people.[11]

The three represents indicated an important shift in party philosophy, party composition, and party organization. At the 16th party congress in 2002, the three represents were added to the CCP Constitution. Jiang took the bold step of leading the CCP to recognize the crucial role of the so-called new social strata as the most dynamic force in China's economic development. The new social strata included groups created during the process of market reform and internationalization, most importantly, private entrepreneurs, managers, and technical staff working for foreign enterprises, as well as professionals, intellectuals, and others who were self-employed or working outside the public sector of the economy. The three represents theory was an ideological rationalization for allowing members of these strata to join the CCP.[12]

Deng Xiaoping is often called the architect of China's reform. It might be reasonable to argue that Jiang Zemin is the engineer who put Deng's design in practice. Under Jiang, the party became more professional, more institutionalized, and more deeply rooted as a governing party. When Jiang was first brought to Beijing from Shanghai in 1989, he made stability a priority. When Deng became increasingly impatient about the slow pace of reform and opening, Deng took a southern tour in 1992 to push for deeper reform and wider opening. Facing the danger of losing Deng's trust and support, Jiang quickly embraced Deng's program of deep reform and took bold measures toward marketization.

After many years of difficult negotiations, China joined the World Trade Organization (WTO) in 2001. This was a milestone in China's transition to the market and its integration into the world economy. The WTO membership has also enabled China to conduct comprehensive administrative and legal reforms in order to conform to the requirements of the market economy and free trade. China's reform policies under Jiang were in favor of the coastal and better-developed regions.

The gap between regions grew significantly. Official corruption became more rampant, and party ideology continued to decline. Under the slogan of stability as a priority, the Public Security Police and the People's Armed Police Force grew significantly in China. The cost of maintaining stability kept going up. Contrary to the wishes of the officials, however, popular unrest and resistance were becoming more widespread. The party leaders perceived growing social tensions and potential threats to sociopolitical stability.

Jiang is often criticized for lack of imagination and bold initiatives. Future historians, however, might judge him more kindly, because Jiang was able to maintain political stability while China was undergoing some very profound social and economic transitions. The pace of China's rise in the world economy accelerated during his rule.

As chairman of the Central Military Commission, Jiang put more emphasis on maintaining the military's loyalty to the party. The defense budget received double-digit annual increases in the Jiang era. Under Jiang's orders, the People's Liberation Army (PLA) disengaged from commercial activities to focus on building a modern military able to fight and win a "limited war under high-tech conditions."[13]

The power transition from Jiang to Hu Jintao was remarkably smooth, compared with previous top leadership transitions. For instance, Mao Zedong's first officially designated successor, Liu Shaoqi, was forced out of power in 1966 during the Cultural Revolution and soon died in prison. Then Lin Biao was written into the CCP Constitution as Mao's successor. But Lin died in an airplane crash after a failed attempt to assassinate Mao in 1971. Mao's last appointed successor, Hua Guofeng, was only able to stay in power as the top leader for two years. Deng's first and second candidates for leadership succession, Hu Yaobang and Zhao Ziyang, were pushed out of power in 1987 and 1989 respectively. When Jiang was designated as Deng's successor in 1989, many observers thought Jiang might be a transitional leader. It was remarkable that Jiang was able to consolidate power and keep the position of general secretary until 2002 and chairman of the Central Military Commission until 2004. It was widely perceived that Deng Xiaoping actually arranged for Hu Jintao to succeed Jiang. The fact that Hu was able to do that peacefully was a clear indication that the CCP leadership transition has been more institutionalized.

HU JINTAO: SOCIAL HARMONY AND SCIENTIFIC DEVELOPMENT

In 2002 Hu Jintao succeeded Jiang Zemin as general secretary of the CCP. In 2004 Hu replaced Jiang as the chairman of the Central Military Commission and completed the leadership transition. Hu and his close partner Premier Wen Jiabao both served in China's poor and remote areas for many years. They brought different experience and perspectives from Jiang Zemin, who spent more time in the coastal areas and the political center, Beijing.

Before he became party secretary in Guizhou and Tibet, Hu was the secretary of the Chinese Communist Youth League (CCYL). The network of CCYL continues to serve as a power base for Hu. Hu is a populist in the sense of advocating policies that address some of the economic downsides of China's three decades of spectacular growth: inequitable income distribution among people and regions, unemployment, and inadequate public services, particularly health care. Special emphasis is placed on combating rural poverty and narrowing the vast rural-urban gap. The country's very serious environmental problems and the necessity for sustainable development are also high on Hu's agenda. Hu advocated building a harmonious society. The underlying assumption is that unless these issues are addressed, social and political instability will increase and lead to disharmony. China has witnessed a growing number of protests by workers and farmers in recent years.[14]

The scientific outlook on development calls for comprehensive, balanced, and sustainable development. Some farsighted leaders have begun to seriously discuss building an ecological civilization. They realize the danger of single-minded pursuit of a high gross domestic product growth rate. If the environment is damaged and people's health is negatively affected, what good will GDP growth bring to the people? The concept of green GDP has gained some attention. The majority of Chinese leaders, however, still believe in economic growth as the top priority. When a coastal delegation told the party secretary of an inland county that the county should maintain green mountains and clean water, the party secretary responded, "Do you mean that we should remain poor forever?"[15] As the economy develops and people's environmental consciousness grows in the better-off coastal areas, some polluting industries are being moved to the less-developed areas of China.

In addition to achieving smooth transition of power at the party center, the CCP has systematically institutionalized leadership transition at all levels. The majority of Chinese middle-and low-level officials today are relatively young, well educated, and committed to the party's modernization agenda. In fact, whether an official will be promoted is based on his or her loyalty to the party and ability to generate economic growth and maintain social stability. The CCP is building a meritocracy. Official promotion is mostly performance based. Children of former senior leaders, however, continue to enjoy some privilege and advantage over candidates from a common background. For instance, three senior PLA officers were promoted to the position of general in July 2009. They are Deputy Chief Ma Xiaotian of the PLA General Staff (whose father was a former provost of the PLA academy), Political Commissar Liu Yuan of the PLA's Academy of Military Sciences (whose father was former PRC president Liu Shaoqi), and former Political Commissar Zhang Haiyang of the Chengdu Military Area Command (whose father was a former member of the Central Military Commission). Such preferential promotion of candidates with strong family connections has caused resentment among other candidates. Over the long run, such practice will be very counterproductive and not sustainable.

Generally speaking, however, cadre selection and official promotion are more and more based on merit. Due to the growing attraction of the stable and prestigious status of working for the party and state, more and more ambitious young people in China are joining the CCP and participating in the civil service exams. For some key positions, the ratio of candidates taking exams for the positions has exceeded 100 to 1.

There are growing calls for political reform and democratization. Deng Xiaoping discussed the need for political reform in the 1980s. Although he made some serious efforts at restoring normalcy to party life, institutionalizing the party, introducing the retirement system, and shifting the party's top priority to economic development, Deng was not able to complete the tough political reforms. Jiang Zemin continued Deng's emphasis on economic reform over political change and put stability above political reform. Jiang was very cautious about political reform. As a result, the economy grew rapidly, but some political contradictions deepened. Chinese society became more unequal and less harmonious. Successive efforts at curbing official corruption mostly failed to stop the rampant corruption.

Hu Jintao and his allies fully realize that corruption has become a cancer threatening the life of the party-state. Without fundamental political reform, however, China's overly centralized political system—being without effective checks and balances—cannot truly solve the problems of corruption and abuse of power. Reform-minded political analyst Yu Keping has openly argued that "democracy is a good thing."[16] Party School scholars Zhou Tianyong and Wang Changjiang have advocated for political reform to overcome entrenched interests and create a new environment for more open and democratic politics.[17]

Within the leadership, Premier Wen Jiabao has been the most outspoken advocate for political reform. Wen argues that China has to pursue political reform to safeguard its economic health:

> Without the safeguarding of political restructuring, China may lose what it has already achieved through economic restructuring and the targets of its modernization drive might not be reached. People's democratic rights and legitimate rights must be guaranteed. People should be mobilized and organized to deal with, in accordance with the law, state, economic, social and cultural affairs.[18]

Wen also wants to "create conditions" to allow the people to criticize and supervise the government as a way to address "the problem of over-concentration of power with ineffective supervision."[19] Wen's comments reflect the growing concern that corruption and abuse may hinder economic development, unless the CCP takes initiative to be held accountable. During his tour of the Shenzhen special economic zone, Wen emphasized that reform and opening is

> the only road to achieving national prosperity and the people's happiness. Regression and stagnation will not only end the achievements of the three-decade old reform and opening-up drive and the rare opportunity of development, but also suffocate the vitality of China's socialist cause with her own characteristics.[20]

So far, Wen's call for broader political reform has met strong resistance from the entrenched interests in Beijing. It is unclear how much progress

Hu and Wen will be able to make in their remaining terms. Hu is going to step down as general secretary of the CCP in 2012 and PRC president in 2013. Wen's second term as premier will expire in 2013.

The Hu-Wen administration first gained high marks in confronting the 2003 severe acute respiratory syndrome (SARS) crisis, when they broke traditional secrecy and allowed some transparency in crisis management. After some initial hesitation they took bold measures, including the firing of the vice mayor of Beijing and the health minister. They demanded country-wide, accurate accounting of SARS cases and timely treatment of infected patients. They also received popular support for their timely responses to natural disasters, including flood and earthquake.

Under Hu's leadership, the Chinese economy has continued to grow rapidly. In 2010, China exceeded Japan as the second-largest economy in the world. In 2008, Beijing successfully hosted the Summer Olympic Games. The Expo 2010 Shanghai was also a spectacular success. Both international events greatly enhanced China's profile in the world community. Inside China, however, there were discussions about the value of hosting such multibillion-dollar international events when there are still large numbers of Chinese citizens struggling to meet the challenges of education, healthcare, and housing. The majority of the Chinese people do take pride in Beijing and Shanghai playing host to such great international events. It is reasonable to say that Chinese nationalism has reached a new height.

Fueled by the new wave of nationalism, some scholars are calling for China to demand more rights in the international community. A book whose title translates to *China Is Not Happy* was written by five nationalistic scholars. The book stems from a few days' conversation with a group of "neo-leftists," and the authors stand accused of whipping up a jingoistic frenzy for the purpose of selling books. In China, the left wing is considered "conservative," while the right wing equals "liberal." The five authors of this book, mostly academics in their forties and fifties, expressed dismay at the rampant "liberalism" among their peers. They view those "liberal elites" as importers of Western ideas and practices, which they say have caused the wealth gap that exists in China, among other sins. On the other hand, they have found a new hope in the young, especially those born after 1980, who have been at the forefront of a reawakening of China's nationalist sentiments. The rise of the left is the result of frustration. The young are upset because they are thrust into a free-market, cutthroat world of fierce competition and long for the days when an iron rice bowl was guaranteed. The middle-aged, the authors included, suffered bouts of disappointment when their blind adoration of the West in the 1980s was dashed by a string of events that turned them from pro-West to anti-West. Now they see themselves as spokesmen of the new generation, whose voices are not taken seriously by the "liberal elite." The truth is, China can be happy when its people enjoy greater wealth, more freedom, and better lives in every way.[21]

One of the biggest challenges will be to bring the political system more into line with the economic system. That effort will involve deep institutional reforms in all sectors. The role of the CCP in daily governance needs to be clarified, with greater separation between the party and the state. That does not mean that the CCP will have no role to play. In some cases, the party is the only entity with the ability to break deadlocks in the power struggle between central and local governments, different regions, or different state organs. Nevertheless, the proper role of the CCP needs to be reconsidered and formalized in a way consistent with the principle of legality and the requirements of rule of law. The legislative system would benefit from further professionalization, with full-time rather than part-time delegates in the NPC and local people's congresses. The experimentation with local elections should continue by elections being allowed at increasingly higher levels of government. The administrative system needs to be improved to ensure that government officials are more accountable to the public.[22]

Harmonious society is a dream rooted in Chinese cultural tradition. It also meets today's popular demand, because many people are living under the enormous pressure created by the grand transitions to modernization and urbanization. If the CCP is going to survive the transition, it also must change with the times, making itself a governing party that is able to meet the unprecedented challenges of a complex and dynamic modern economy and society. The scientific development outlook is an ambitious effort to meet such challenges. There are still tensions between the economy-first policy and the pro-people policy. Central to the pro-people policy is addressing head-on the problems of poverty and regional inequality. It remains to be seen whether the Chinese party-state can successfully rise to the challenges of modernization.

Chapter 4

State Institutions and Policy Making

THE NATIONAL PEOPLE'S CONGRESS

In constitutional principle, the National People's Congress (NPC) is the highest organ of power in China. In reality, the Chinese Communist Party (CCP) leadership holds the real power.

The NPC elects the president of the People's Republic of China (PRC) and approves the appointment of the premier based on the recommendation of the president. Empowered by the Constitution, the NPC has broad power and responsibilities. The NPC normally meets for about two weeks each spring. The Standing Committee of the NPC has about 150 members. When the NPC is not in session, its power is exercised by its Standing Committee.

The NPC was formed in 1954, and it passed the first Constitution in its founding meeting. That Constitution represented the beginning of institutionalization of the PRC political system. Although the Constitution claimed that all power belonged to the people and the highest organ of power in the country was the NPC, the CCP in fact became more and more dominant. Mao Zedong and other key leaders insisted that the CCP leadership was the core of the Chinese political system. The NPC normally approved decisions made by the CCP leadership without major changes.

Between 1964 and 1974, there was no election of people's deputies and no meeting of the NPC. The NPC ceased to function during the Cultural Revolution. Many former NPC leaders were persecuted in the political turmoil. China's political institutionalization suffered a serious setback. At the 1975 meeting of the NPC, Premier Zhou

The Great Hall of the People, where the most important national political conferences meet. (Photograph taken by Guoli Liu.)

declared China's ambitious goal of modernization. But Zhou was suffering from cancer, and the leadership was divided about China's development strategy.

It was not until Deng Xiaoping resumed top party leadership in 1978 that the NPC system entered a new period of development. In 1979, a new electoral law was passed. In 1980, direct elections were held for people's deputies to fill county congress seats. At Peking University, for instance, a competitive election was held for one deputy to the Haidian district congress of people's deputies in Beijing. Many voters thought that direct election represented the future of China's democratic politics. But still by 2011, direct elections have not developed beyond the county level. It may take a long time for China to develop truly competitive democratic elections at the provincial and national levels.

In 1982, a new Constitution was passed by the NPC. The power of the NPC was gradually expanded. Just as the National Congress of the CCP elects party leaders every five years, the NPC elects a new state leadership in a meeting a few months following the party congress. In theory, the NPC delegates elect all key state leaders, including the president, the vice president, the chairman of the Central Military Commission, the chief justice, and the chief prosecutor. In reality, all of the candidates for the most important positions are nominated by the CCP leadership in advance. The party also issues guidelines for NPC elections. The CCP and its Organization Department control the selections of NPC delegates and recommend candidates for key leadership positions. For instance, the Politburo Standing Committee recommends the candidates for president of the PRC, chairman of the PRC Central Military Commission, chairman and vice chairman of the NPC national committee, and premier of the State Council. The NPC elects or approves the candidates. The formal election process is hardly competitive. When Hu Jintao was elected to his second term as PRC president in 2008, the vote was 2,956 for, 3 against, and 5 abstaining.[1]

The organizational principle of the NPC is democratic centralism, which is also the organizational principle of the CCP. This principle requires that the minority obey the majority, lower-level organization obey higher-level organization, and the whole party obey the central leadership. The CCP leadership of the NPC is realized through party control of policies and personnel.

The 1982 Constitution has been amended several times. The phrases "rule of law," "socialist market economy," "private property," and "human rights" are now all written into the Constitution. There is a growing movement toward constitutionalism. Some legal experts advocate that all individuals and political organizations in China must follow the Constitution. If the Constitution enjoys supreme authority, the rule of law will take root. That rooting requires the CCP to operate within the Constitution as well. Only the NPC can amend the Constitution. A Constitutional amendment can be proposed by the NPC Standing Committee or one-fifth of the members of the NPC. An amendment can be passed if it receives the approval of two-thirds of the total NPC deputies.

The NPC is becoming more powerful in the reform era. Peng Zhen was a former party leader of Beijing who was persecuted during the Cultural Revolution. When he became the chairman of the NPC Standing Committee in 1983, Peng was determined to make the NPC more powerful, in order to prevent the lawless situation of the Cultural Revolution from happening again. Peng's successors Wan Li

National People's Congress chairman Wu Bangguo delivers a work report during a plenary session of the National People's Congress in Beijing, China, March 9, 2010. (AP Photo/Ng Han Guan.)

(chairman of the NPC Standing Committee from 1988 to 1993) and Qiao Shi (chairman from 1993 to 1998) also advocated a stronger role for the NPC in China's political life. Qiao maintained a strong voice for promoting the rule of law.

Since 1998, the second-ranking leader in the CCP leadership has been the chairman of the NPC Standing Committee. Li Peng (1998–2003) and Wu Bangguo (2003 to the present) have both been very influential leaders inside the party-state. Each of them was ranked only behind the general secretary of the CCP. At the provincial level and lower levels, more and more party secretaries have also begun serving as chairmen of the people's congresses at their respective levels. Such arrangements on the one hand have strengthened party leadership. On the other hand, they also have had the effect of strengthening the people's congresses versus other political organizations, including the respective administrative organs.

Representative democracy is the wave of the future. According to constitutional scholar Cai Dingjian, representative democracy is the only way to provide legitimacy for the government. There is no alternative.[2] The National People's Congress can play an even more substantial and significant role in Chinese politics in the future. The NPC supervises the work of the State Council, the Supreme People's Court (SPC), and the Supreme People's Procuratorate (SPP). The State Council, the SPC, and the SPP all report to the NPC during its annual meeting. The NPC deputies pay close attention to national economic development planning and national budgets. In recent years, many NPC deputies have expressed their disapproval of the anticorruption work of the SPC and SPP.

At the provincial level, in most cases the CCP secretary also serves as the chairman of the provincial people's congress. Such practice has strengthened the authority of the provincial people's congress. However, separation of the party and state remains a tough issue to resolve. In the 1980s, Deng Xiaoping proposed separation of the party and state as a key step of political reform. In reality, the party and state remain highly intertwined. The top party leader is still the top official at each level, from the county to the province, and then to the center. There is no doubt that the CCP is firmly in control of the Chinese political system.

CHINESE PEOPLE'S POLITICAL CONSULTATIVE CONFERENCE

The Chinese People's Political Consultative Conference (CPPCC) is a political advisory body, consisting of delegates from a range of political parties and organizations, as well as independent members. Apart from the CCP, there are eight democratic parties in China. They are the Revolutionary Committee of the Chinese Kuomintang, the China Democratic League, the China Democratic National Construction Association, the China Association for Promoting Democracy, the Chinese Peasants' and Workers' Democratic Party, the China Zhi Gong Dang, the Jiu San Society, and the Taiwan Democratic Self-Government League. The largest and dominant party in the conference is the CCP. Other members are drawn from the united front parties allied with the CCP and from independent members who do not belong to any party.

Mao Zedong served as the founding chairman of the CPPCC from 1949 to 1954. From 1954 to 1976, Zhou Enlai was the chairman. During the Cultural Revolution, from 1966 to 1976; however, the CPPCC stopped functioning, and it did not resume work until 1978. Deng Xiaoping served as the third chairman from 1978 to 1983. He was succeeded by Deng Yingchao, serving from 1983 to 1988; Li Xiannian, serving from 1988 to 1992; and Li Ruihuan, serving from 1993 to 2003. Since 2003, the CPPCC chairman has been Jia Qinglin, who is the fourth-ranking CCP Politburo Standing Committee member. Jia's second term will end in 2013. The current CPPCC has 26 vice chairpersons.

The CPPCC has several special committees, including the Committee for Handling Proposals; the Committee for Economic Affairs; the Committee of Population, Resources, and Environment; the Committee of Education, Science, Culture, Health, and Sports; the Committee for Social and Legal Affairs; the Committee for Ethnic and Religious Affairs; the Committee of Cultural and Historical Data; the Committee for Affairs of Hong Kong, Macao, Taiwan Compatriots, and Overseas Chinese; and the Committee for Foreign Affairs.

The CPPCC began as a very powerful organ. Most of its power was transferred to the NPC in 1954. Both the NPC and the CPPCC were pushed aside by the radical leaders in power during the Cultural Revolution (1966–1976). Since the end of the Cultural Revolution and the beginning of reform, both the NPC and the CPPCC have restored their regular meetings and strengthened their institutional capacities.

Belonging to an advisory body without direct administrative responsibilities, members of the CPPCC should have a great degree of autonomy to critically examine government policies and provide critical comments and suggestions for improving government work. Some CPPCC members, however, only perform ceremonial roles

Delegates gather for the opening ceremony of the Chinese People's Political Consultative Conference (CPPCC) in Beijing's Great Hall of the People March 3, 2005. The CPPCC is a top advisory body in China. (AP Photo/Greg Baker.)

without any critical spirit. CPPCC member Ni Ping claimed that she never voted against any resolutions because of her patriotism. Such a comment reflects a lack of independent spirit found among some current members of the CPPCC. Over the long run the NPC, as the highest organ of the state with a focus on legislative power, and the CPPCC, as the top advisory body, can both play a significant role in China's political system. However, due to the highly centralized structure of power and its domination by the CCP, the power and potential of the NPC and CPPCC are far from realized.

STATE COUNCIL: ADMINISTRATIVE REFORMS

The State Council is the administrative authority of the PRC. It is headed by the premier and includes the heads of governmental ministries and key agencies. According to the 1982 Constitution, the State Council is composed of the following: the premier, the vice premiers, the state councillors, the ministers in charge of ministries, the ministers in charge of commissions, the auditor-general, and the secretary-general. The premier has overall responsibility for the State Council. The ministers have overall responsibility for the respective ministries or commissions under their charge.

The current structure of the State Council was put in place in 2003, as a result of a program of central government consolidation and simplification. China's ministries are vertical administrative institutions with three or four main tiers: central offices in Beijing and bureaus in provinces, prefectures, and counties. The number, type, and relative importance of the ministries have varied over time in a pattern reflective of the policy emphases of the day. There are currently 28 ministries and commissions. At present, all but two of the ministers belong to the CCP. The exceptions are the minister of science and technology, Wan Gang, and the minister of health, Chen Zhu.

The key ministries include foreign affairs, state security, public security, education, finance, justice, transport, commerce, agriculture, culture, railways, civil affairs, science and technology, water resources, environmental protection, housing and urban-rural construction, and labor. The key commissions are national development and reform, national population and family planning, and state ethnic affairs. In principle, commissions have a more comprehensive function than ministries, and some are intended to coordinate the work of several former ministries. Although there is a Ministry of Defense, the State Council does not have direct control over the military. The Chinese military is controlled by the Central Military Commission of the CCP.

There are more than one dozen other organizations directly under the State Council, including the State-Owned Assets Supervision and Administration Commission, the General Administration of Customs, the State Administration of Taxation, the State Administration for Industry and Commerce, the National Bureau of Statistics, the State Administration for Religious Affairs, and the National Bureau of Corruption Prevention.

The State Council has experienced several rounds of restructuring. A key objective of the restructuring has been to reduce the size of the bureaucracy. Like all bureaucracies, however, the State Council and its ministries have a strong tendency to expand again after each restructuring. Contemporary China has a greater number of government officials than any previous era in Chinese history. Administrative expenses of government departments have been increasing by more than 100 billion yuan a year since 2005, hitting nearly 1,100 billion yuan (about $167 billion) in 2009 and accounting for about 30 percent of the overall fiscal revenue, with an annual growth of 23 percent. The bulging government costs not only add to people's tax burden but are also a misuse of limited funds to improve people's livelihood. The international standard for the share of administrative cost in overall fiscal expenditure is about 5 percent. If the central government can lower its cost to the international level and if the public can begin supervising the use of the money thus saved, more funds can find their way to medical service, education, and social securities.[3] The growth of bureaucracy is not just

Zhou Enlai served as China's premier from 1949 to 1976. (Bettmann/Corbis.)

an issue concerning the central government. All levels of Chinese government face the challenges of controlling the size of growing staff.

The premier is in charge of the administrative work of the government. Zhou Enlai served as the first premier, holding that position from the founding of the PRC in 1949 until his death in 1976. Zhou was an extremely skillful political leader and played an important role in almost all key aspects of Chinese politics. From 1949 to 1958, Zhou also concurrently served as China's foreign minister. He was a strong advocate for peaceful coexistence. Zhou Enlai was a very popular leader in China, who also enjoyed widespread respect around the world. When Zhou died, Mao Zedong named Hua Guofeng as the premier. In 1980 Hua was replaced by Zhao Ziyang, who served as premier to 1987. Zhao was a strong supporter and effective implementer of Deng Xiaoping's reform and opening policy. He helped to move China from its command economy to a market economy. Zhao's theoretical contribution included the "preliminary stage of socialism," which promoted a mixed economy over the long run. Zhao's successor was the more conservative Li Peng. In 1998 Zhu Rongji succeeded Li as premier.

Chinese premier Wen Jiabao greets those attending the opening plenary of the World Economic Forum in Dalian, China, September 10, 2009. (AP Photo/Elizabeth Dalziel.)

Zhu was the tough and effective premier who led state-owned enterprises reform and China's entry into the World Trade Organization. Since 2003, Wen Jiabao has been China's premier. Wen has developed a reputation for being a populist who cares about more balanced growth and social harmony. He has played a critical role in managing China's response to the global financial crisis. The massive stimulus plan has significantly contributed to China's quick recovery and rapid economic growth. In 2010, China's gross domestic product (GDP) grew by 10 percent, and its GDP exceeded that of Japan to turn China into the second-largest economy in the world.

CENTRAL MILITARY COMMISSION

The Central Military Commission (CMC) is the leadership organ for the People's Liberation Army (PLA). Nominally there are two organizations: the Central Military Commission of the People's Republic of China (a state organ) and the Central Military Commission of the Communist Party of China (a party organ). However, the two organizations are identical in membership; thus there is only one de facto Central Military Commission. The command and control of the PLA is exercised by the 12-man CMC.

Mao Zedong first gained control of the CCP military in 1935, during the Long March, and he kept his leadership position until his death in 1976. Hua Guofeng was a transitional chairman of the CMC from 1976 to 1981, but Vice Chairman Deng Xiaoping gained effective control of the CMC in 1979. Deng served as the chairman from 1981 to 1989. Jiang Zemin was the CMC chairman from 1989 to 2004. The current CMC chairman is Hu Jintao, who is also general secretary of the CCP and president of the PRC. The election of the party CMC always takes place before the election of the state CMC. For instance, Xi Jinping was first selected by the CCP Central Committee as the vice chairman of the party CMC, and then he was elected by the National People's Congress Standing Committee (NPCSC) as the vice chairman of the state CMC in 2010. It is an unwritten rule that the de facto top CCP leader also serves as chairman of the CMC. That is why Xi's recent appointment as vice chairman of the CMC has been widely perceived as a critical step in the leadership transition scheduled to take place at the 2012 CCP National Congress.

The PLA headquarters has four departments: the General Staff Department, the General Political Department, the General Logistics Department, and the General Armaments Department. The CMC exercises leadership over the seven military regions and over the navy, the air force, and the Second Artillery (a strategic missile force) through the four general departments. The seven military regions are Beijing, Shenyang, Lanzhou, Jinan, Nanjing, Guangzhou, and Chengdu. In the 1980s, 1 million PLA troops were demobilized as a result of China's decisive move to focus on economic development. In the Jiang era, the size of the PLA was reduced by another half-million troops. China's armed forces remain the world's largest, with over 2 million members. The recent focus has been on building a smaller, better-educated, disciplined, well-trained, and well-equipped military. A growing number of college graduates are being recruited to join the PLA.

ADMINISTRATIVE DIVISIONS OF THE COUNTRY

The Constitution of the PRC provides three administrative levels below the central government: province, county, and township. The provincial units of China include 23 provinces, 5 autonomous regions, 4 centrally administered municipalities, and 2 special administrative regions. The provinces include Hebei, Shanxi, Liaoning, Jilin, Heilongjiang, Jiangsu, Zhejiang, Anhui, Fujian, Jiangxi, Shandong, Henan, Hubei, Hunan, Guangdong, Hainan, Sichuan, Guizhou, Yunnan, Shaanxi, Gansu, Qinghai, and Taiwan (which is not under Beijing's control).

An autonomous region is defined as being a provincial-level area with a high population of a minority ethnic or cultural group. The five groups forming autonomous regions are the Tibetans in Tibet, the Zhuang in Guangxi, the Uyghur in Xinjiang, the Mongols in Inner Mongolia, and the Huis in Ningxia. Most of their local officials are drawn from the minority populations, the minority languages are used in government and education, and the ethnic minority populations are exempt from the one-child policy. The party secretary of an autonomous region is usually a Han, however, rather than an ethnic minority. Xinjiang, Tibet, and Inner Mongolia are the three largest regions in China. The ethnic minorities account for about 8 percent of China's 1.33 billion people. Only in China can groups of over 100 million people be called "the minorities."

There are four "centrally administered municipalities," which are Beijing, Shanghai, Tianjin, and Chongqing. They are high-level cities that are directly under the central government, with status equal to that of the provinces. The party secretaries of the four cities are Politburo members. They are more powerful than most of the provincial party secretaries, who are normally members of the CCP Central Committee. Beijing is the capital city, and it is China's political, cultural, and financial center. Tianjin is a large, industrial northern coastal city with a growing high technology sector. Shanghai is China's most advanced commercial and industrial center. It also desires to become a financial center in Asia. Its Pudong district has become China's showcase of dynamic economic growth. Chongqing is a new centrally administered city founded in 2000. It has 30 million people and is undergoing unprecedented industrialization and urbanization. In May 2010, Chongqing's Liangjiang district was designated by the State Council as a new special economic zone. It enjoys preferential policies similar to

Shanghai Pudong has enjoyed extraordinary growth since the early 1990s. (Photograph taken by Guoli Liu.)

those of Shanghai's Pudong district and Tianjin's Binhai district. Liang-jiang district will be a testing ground for new financial, tax, investment, trade, and land policies.

Hong Kong and Macao are special administrative regions (SARs). Deng Xiaoping proposed "one country, two systems." The idea has been put into practice in managing the SARs. That means socialism for mainland China and capitalism for Hong Kong and Macao. Hong Kong and Macao enjoy a high degree of autonomy, including a greater level of executive and legislative power than China's provinces. For instance, the chief executive of Hong Kong is elected by an 800-member election committee in Hong Kong and then appointed by the central Chinese government. The chief executive of Macao is selected by a 300-member election committee in Macao and then appointed by the central Chinese government. In contrast, the CCP Central Committee directly controls the selection of the governors in the provinces. Each SAR also has its own currency. Foreign affairs and defense are managed by the central Chinese government.

CENTRAL-LOCAL RELATIONS IN TRANSITION

China's political power remains highly centralized. The party center retains the right to appoint local officials, including all key provincial leaders. Constitutionally, there is no federalism in the PRC. China remains a unitary state, in which the center maintains firm control over key personnel and political and economic decisions. Nevertheless, with deepening reform and opening, China's political system in terms of central-local relations is functioning more and more on federalist lines.[4]

Certain powers are vested in the superior level over its subordinates. The most important among these is the power to appoint and dismiss officials. The government at each level also reserves the power to draw up budgets and levy taxes in its subordinate units. The central government reserves the power to allocate and redistribute resources among the provinces; provincial governments do the same for counties and cities. Tax revenues from well-off provinces are reallocated to help less well-off regions.[5] Sometimes local officials can thwart central directives by inaction. In practice, the center-local relationship can be thought of as a kind of power grid, in which the vertical elements are the bureaucratic departments of the central systems and the horizontal elements are the provinces and cities. In some instances, the vertical and horizontal elements work at cross-purposes, stymieing rather than facilitating political activity.[6]

In the beginning of reform and opening, in the late 1970s and early 1980s, the emphasis was decentralization. There are growing demands from the provincial and local governments for more autonomy. Having grown accustomed to a greater degree of autonomy, the provinces now tend to resist any effort by the central government to recoup its control of local affairs. The center, for its part, believes that the most important problems confronting the economy can best be addressed at the national level. Since the mid-1990s, however, there has been increased emphasis on strengthening the center's authority and raising central tax revenue.

China's central government has had a habit of enacting laws and regulations that require local government action but providing no funds to cover the costs. For example, the central government, wanting to improve the quality of air and water, has put in place a full set of environmental laws and regulations, but it gives little or no financial support to local governments to cover the costs of enforcing them. In education and health care, too, the central government enacts programs for expansion and improvement but relies on the local governments for the funds to carry out these mandates.[7] Although Beijing is not willing to reduce its control over the provincial governments, it is likely that China's provinces will grow more autonomous as their economic powers increase and as popular demand for political participation grows.

In an integrated, multilevel, nationwide bureaucratic system, China must mesh both vertical (coordination from center to locality) and horizontal (coordination within a given geographic area) requirements. Chinese government administration is primarily carried out by two different kinds of institutions: vertically organized ministries and horizontally organized regional governments. The Chinese use vivid terminology to describe their crisscrossing jurisdictions: the vertical bureaucracies are called lines (*tiao*), while the horizontal coordinating bodies at various levels are called pieces (*kuai*). The relationship between the vertical and horizontal bodies is called *tiao/kuai guanxi*. Chinese officials at a middle or lower level have a number of bosses in different places of *tiao* and *kuai*. It becomes important in these circumstances to determine which of these bosses has priority over others. It is in this sense that political scientist Kenneth Lieberthal describes the Chinese polity as "fragmented authoritarianism."[8] Most officials tend to report first to their superiors who hold the power of appointment and supervision. The CCP's organization department at each level controls the appointment power for officials below that level. When there are confusions or conflicts about authority relations among different organs, it is often up to the party committee one level above to clarify matters.

POLICY MAKING AND IMPLEMENTATION

The most important political and economic decisions in China are made by the CCP. According to the textbook description of the party-government relationship in China's political system, the party proposes, and the government disposes; the party makes policy, and the government carries it out. In real organizations, however, things seldom function according to the textbook, and the line separating policy making from policy implementation is often difficult to draw. It is important to note that all the key party leaders also occupy senior positions in the government. The CCP has two means for ensuring that its policies are implemented by government officials. First, it has the power of appointment, since at each governmental level, appointments are the responsibility of the party organization at the level just above. Provincial officials are appointed by the central party organization; provincial party organizations in turn appoint officials at the county and city levels. Second, the performance of those officials appointed by the party is then monitored by party agencies.[9]

There has been growing attention to scientific decision making. Officials are required to study modern knowledge of decision making and public administration. Mao Zedong used to advocate the "mass" line of policy making. According to Mao, correct ideas and effective policy should come from the masses and then be put into practice. In his early years, Mao paid close attention to social investigation and survey. He was able to rely on collective wisdom to make effective policies. In his late years, however, Mao became more and more detached from the masses. He also became increasingly distrustful of his colleagues. As a result, Mao often made big decisions without close consultation with members of the Politburo. In fact, the Central Cultural Revolution

Group (CCRG) selected by Mao effectively became the most important decision-making body during the Cultural Revolution. The CCRG consisted mainly of radical supporters of Mao, including his wife, Jiang Qing, along with Kang Sheng, Yao Wenyuan, and Zhang Chunqiao. The CCRG had a central role to play in the Cultural Revolution's first two years, and for a short period of time the group replaced the Politburo Standing Committee as the de facto power organ of the CCP. This was not consistent with the CCP Constitution. When personal rule replaced collective leadership, disasters and chaos became the norm rather than the exception.

When Deng Xiaoping returned to power in 1977, he condemned the radical approach of arbitrary decision making during the Cultural Revolution. Deng emphasized the normalization of party and state institutions. In principle, Deng stressed collective leadership over personal rule. In reality, Deng was not able to resist the desire to allow the party core (meaning himself) to have the final decision-making power on the most important issues.

Returning to the tradition of "seeking truth from facts," Deng and his supporters adopted the "trial and error" approach in reform and opening. The experimental approach worked well in the cases of the agricultural household responsibility system and the special economic zones (SEZs). The agriculture reform began with spontaneous peasant initiatives and was expanded to the whole country after its proven success in Anhui and Sichuan Provinces. The SEZs in Shenzhen, Shantou, Xiamen, and Zhuhai became testing grounds for important economic and trade policies. The successful policies were later expanded to other open cities on the Chinese coast, and the policies that worked well in the open cities were later adopted by other regions of China.

The role of think tanks has been growing in China. The Chinese Academy of Social Sciences reports directly to the State Council. Each provincial unit also has its own academy of social sciences. China's universities and other key organizations have established a large number of research institutions. Many research institutions are trying to conduct research projects that have policy relevance. This is particularly true in the area of economic development. For instance, the China Center for Economic Research at Peking University has become a critical center of education and research. Several previous members of the center are now serving in China's central bank, ministry of finance, and other key institutions. Justin Yifu Lin, the center's founder and first director, is now senior vice president and chief economist of the World Bank.

The CCP used to be a highly centralized party with strong discipline. The party center's policies were quickly implemented. In recent years, however, the party has lost its past ideological appeal and loosened party discipline. There have been increasing complaints that central orders often have not been implemented outside of Zhongnanhai (where the CCP central leadership and State Council are located). Of course, such complaints about the weakening center are overstated. In reality, the CCP central leadership continues to exercise an enormous amount of power and influence in every major political, social, and economic arena.

With less ideological purity and a more complex bureaucratic machine, the abuse of power is becoming more widespread than ever before. There has been significant growth of coercive power. The coercive organs of power have been expanding quickly. Urban administrative enforcement sometimes has become violent and led to popular resistance. The increasing number of cases involving demolition of old housing and urban construction have created unprecedented popular discontent and sometimes led to violent confrontations between the authorities and the citizens.

Government and citizen relations are becoming less harmonious than desired. "Contradictions among people" are growing quickly in China's transitional society. The "scientific development" outlook aims to create a balance between the state and society. The leadership also realizes that China cannot single-mindedly pursue economic development only. It is time to conduct more substantial political and administrative reform, in order to satisfy popular demand for political participation and enhance people's living standards. The evaluation of China's policy making and implementation is increasingly performance based.

Over the long run, it is most likely that China will develop a modern bureaucracy based on democratic ideals and meritocracy. In December 2010, 1.4 million college-educated Chinese young people took the National Public Service Exam. They were competing for 16,000 positions in the central party departments, state ministries, and other central agencies. In one case, 4,961 people contended for a single post offered by the National Energy Administration.[10] Such intense competition is likely to increase the talent pool of China's future decision makers. At the same time, the large number of civil service exam takers might also reflect the lack of other equally attractive employment opportunities for well-educated and ambitious young people. China needs to further develop a modern human resource system that can offer more abundant opportunities for its citizens.

The authoritarian decision making has enabled China to make timely decisions on many issues, including large construction projects such as a national highway system and the high-speed railway. Without effective checks and balances, however, it could be disastrous if the center were to make any serious mistakes. In order to meet the growing challenges of managing a complex modernizing economy and transitional society, China must modernize its party-state institutions and decision-making mechanisms. Without substantial political reforms, it will be difficult to preserve and advance the gains of economic reforms. In next chapter, we will examine China's economic development and social policy.

Chapter 5

Economic Development and Social Policy

THE CHINA DREAM: WEALTH AND POWER

Wealth and power have been the core elements of China's dream for over a century. Since the 1911 revolution, successive generations of Chinese have searched for different paths to realize this dream. It wasn't until after the Cultural Revolution that Chinese leaders finally embraced modernization through reform, rather than revolution. One of the most positive results of China's economic reform has been the dramatic drop in the number of people living in extreme destitution. In 1980, 76 percent of rural Chinese lived on less than the equivalent of one dollar a day; by 1988 the percentage had plummeted to 23 percent, and by 2003 only 9 percent lived with such hardship. Measured by the World Bank's "international poverty line" of people living on less than $1.25 a day at 2005 purchasing power parity (PPP), China's poverty population declined from 835 million people in 1981 to 683 million in 1990, 447 million in 1999, and 208 million in 2005.[1] It is truly remarkable that over 600 million Chinese people have been able to escape from poverty in the last three decades.

Since the late 1970s, Deng Xiaoping's vision of reform and opening has allowed China to modernize rapidly. Deng stressed that the top priority should be improving people's living standard. The right to govern has to be earned. Economic development provides legitimacy to the government. In contrast, poverty undermines regime legitimacy. The past claims of ideological purity simply could not stand the test of time as poverty persisted. Deng strongly urged China's leaders to stop ideology debates in order to focus on modernization. Since reform and opening began in 1978, China's search for modernity has entered a new stage with an accelerated pace. Change in Chinese politics is inevitable. But as the Tiananmen crisis in 1989 illustrated, Chinese reformers have learned the importance of change amid stability. Stability can only be achieved through timely, fundamental, and well-managed change. Politics in a rising China are qualitatively different from politics in a revolutionary China. China's reform and opening have reached a deeper stage.[2] Internal conflicts and tensions have developed to such a degree that fundamental political reforms are necessary. Without profound political change and deeper reform, the peaceful rise of China will be an unfulfilled dream. The paradox of Chinese politics today can only be solved via a combination of socioeconomic development and political reform. Deng Xiaoping's approach of economic liberalization and political control has reached a critical point. Institutional, ideological, and elite changes are required for China to reach a higher level of development.

Under the policy of reform and opening, China has enjoyed rapid economic growth for over three decades. The gross domestic product (GDP) annual growth rate increased from approximately 4 percent prior to the reform (1952–1977) to near 10 percent during 1978–2010. Based on PPP data from the World Bank, China's overall output growth lagged dramatically behind Japanese performance from 1950 to 1977. In 1952, China's GDP was 78.5 percent of that of Japan. By 1978, China's GDP had declined to 38.5 percent of Japan's. As China's economy took off under reform, its GDP reached 70.5 percent of Japan's in 1990 and jumped to 219.2 percent of the Japanese GDP by 2004. From 1978 to 2004, China's GDP grew from 13.6 percent to 64 percent of that of the United States. From 1978 to 2004, China's per capita GDP, as a percentage of that of the United States, grew from 3.2 percent to 15.7 percent.[3] In 2010, China's GDP based on the exchange rate reached $6 trillion, exceeding that of Japan for the first time. At the same time, it is important to remember that China's per capita GDP is only about one-tenth of that of Japan or the United States. China is still a developing country with unbalanced growth and unequal distribution of income.

In comparative perspective, China's economy has been growing very rapidly, and its politics in the post-Mao era have been relatively stable.

Social tensions have been rising with growing inequality in personal income and regional disparities. The current leadership under Hu Jintao and Wen Jiabao has made building a harmonious society a top priority. As China moves toward achieving its long-term dream of wealth and power, it is appropriate to review its progress and examine challenges ahead.

GRADUALISM RATHER THAN SHOCK THERAPY

In contrast to the shock therapy method adopted by many Eastern European countries, China adopted an incremental approach to economic reform. Deng Xiaoping described the approach as "crossing the river by feeling stones under feet." Two of the most outstanding features of China's economic transition are the "dual-track" system and "growing out of the plan."[4]

The innovative dual-track system allowed a relatively smooth transition from the fixed price to flexible market price system. Instead of a shock therapy that would suddenly liberalize the price system, China's reformers adopted a dual-track approach in the 1980s—the coexistence of a state-fixed low price for some goods and a market-based floating price for a gradually growing share of goods. This approach helped to ease the pain and shock of marketization while allowing a growing percentage of the economy to move into a market-based system. The drawback of the dual-track system was that it offered enormous opportunity for official speculation on goods in short supply and high demand. This system created loopholes for corrupt officials to enrich themselves at the cost of the public. By controlling scarce material, officials could reap hefty profits by directly or indirectly selling such goods at the higher market prices. As a classical thinker has pointed out, "Power tends to corrupt, and absolute power corrupts absolutely."[5] Official corruption has become a very serious challenge to the legitimacy of the Chinese regime.

Similarly, "growing out of the plan" on one hand eased the pain of economic transition. On the other hand, it left the daunting task of reforming the state-owned enterprises (SOEs) up to future reform efforts. The SOEs continue to take the lion's share of governmental investment but only produce a small and declining portion of China's GDP. Reforming the SOEs has become a key task of China's deep reform.

Incremental reform is conducive to maintaining a balance between the requirements of stability and speed during the reform process. However, incremental reform also has some costs. First, it can be characterized as taking two steps forward and one step back, due to the conflicts between the two sectors of the economy and the alternations of which the sector the government endorses. Second, incremental reform is preconditioned by the existence of the dual-track system or resource allocation instead of by entire reliance on market competition.[6] As Merle Goldman and Roderick MacFarquhar point out:

> The move to the market and the open-door policies that have led to a weakening party-state could in time lead to a freer, more democratic society as China's huge population becomes more prosperous and demands greater rights. At the same time, China's increasing geographic and social inequalities, coupled with rising expectations, also have the potential to lead to massive social upheaval and political instability. Such is the paradox of China's reform.[7]

China's experimental approach to reform originated from the grass-roots level. It was the hungry farmers who decided to divide their land on a family basis. The family-based methods soon proved to be much more productive than the collective farms under the people's communes. The household responsibility system that began in the late 1970s dismantled the people's communes. Peasant families can sign contracts with their village to lease land. After fulfilling the contract by paying tax to the government, they have total control of everything produced on the leased land. The agricultural household responsibility system strongly promoted productivity and improved farmers' livelihood. In the late 1970s to the mid-1980s, peasant household income rose quickly, and the urban-rural divide became smaller. It was a good time for Chinese farmers. As urban reforms accelerated since the mid-1980s, however, income in the cities has been rising faster than in the countryside. Peasants have confronted the challenges of increasing prices for fertilizer and other industrial goods; intense competition of agricultural supplies from other sources, including imports from abroad; and more bureaucratic fees.

Under the old command economy, China's main focus was on self-reliance. The traditional planned economy produced a highly distorted economic structure, leading to irrational allocation of resources. State-fixed prices were often far below market prices and did not reflect the true value of goods and services. As a result, the fixed prices could not play the role of efficiently allocating resources, as they are supposed to do in a market economy. This rigid command system made it impossible for enterprises to respond promptly to the rapidly changing international market. The Cultural Revolution (1966–1976) forced the Chinese economy into total isolation and drove it to the edge of collapse. In 1978, China's share of world trade was only 0.6 percent.[8]

After one decade of rapid economic growth, China's reforms encountered serious obstacles. By 1988 Deng Xiaoping had realized the urgent need for deeper reform. The 3rd Plenary Session of the 13th Chinese Communist Party (CCP) Congress in September 1988 first proposed "comprehensive deep reform." It was not until Deng Xiaoping's southern tour in 1992 that the CCP leadership finally began to gain consensus about the need for deep reform. Deng made it clear that whoever did not support deeper reform and more comprehensive opening should be pushed out of power. Jiang Zemin and other leaders quickly embraced Deng's strategy of reform. They were able to move China out of the temporary retreat from reform after 1989. China's reform entered a new stage of deep reform after 1992.[9]

In the early 1990s, the Chinese yuan was devalued to promote export. From 1994 to 2005, the official exchange rate was maintained around the level of U.S. $1 to 8.3 Chinese yuan. Such an exchange rate plus export tax rebates and other export promotion policies led to a sharp rise in both foreign trade and foreign direct investment (FDI). From 2005 to 2010, however, the value of Chinese yuan has appreciated such that U.S. $1 is worth 6.65 yuan. The United States and other Western countries have put growing pressure on China to raise the value of its currency. Critics believe that the relatively undervalued yuan has allowed China to sell its products at low prices and occupy growing market shares.

China's entry into the World Trade Organization (WTO) in 2001 had positive effects, not only in promoting China's further integration with the world economy, but also in advancing China's domestic legal and economic reforms toward those of a full market economy. Since 2001 China has experience explosive growth in foreign trade. From 2000 to 2010, China's foreign trade grew from $470 billion to $3 trillion.

In 2010, China became the largest exporter in the world and the second-largest trading nation in the world, only behind the United States. This is truly extraordinary, considering the fact that China ranked 32nd with a small trade volume of $20 billion in 1978. China has also become the largest recipient of FDI in the developing world, receiving a total of more than $600 billion. The degree of interdependence between China and the world economy has grown to an unprecedented level. As a result, China has gained multiple benefits, chiefly an accelerated economic growth rate. On the other hand, China has also been exposed to the growing pressures and risks of globalization. The 1997 Asian financial crisis, the 2003 SARS epidemic, and especially the 2008 global financial crisis are examples of the new challenges confronting the Chinese. As China's trade volume has increased dramatically, the components of Chinese exports have also gone through significant changes.

A vital source of China's economic growth in general and trade development in particular is its large, dynamic, and disciplined work-force. China's labor force accounts for 26.3 percent of the world's total workforce. In 2002, China's average wage was only 3.4 percent of Japan's average wage, 2.1 percent of the United States's, 7.8 percent of South Korea's, and 24.4 percent of the Philippines'. Such a large labor force and low labor cost make Chinese labor-intensive exports, such as textiles, extremely competitive in the world market. Chinese clothing exports account for more than 20 percent of the world total.[10] By 2005, the Chinese foreign trade sector directly employed more than 80 million people. Foreign trade has significantly contributed to China's economic growth.

The content of Chinese exports is more important than the speed of export growth. In contrast to what comparative advantage theory would suggest for a country at China's level of development, China exports a great deal of sophisticated consumer electronics. Foreign investors have played a critical role in this industry. While China welcomes foreign investment, it has always encouraged technology transfer and fostered domestic capabilities. Many joint ventures in consumer electronics have achieved great success and contributed to China's exports.[11] In order to achieve sustained trade growth, China should shift away from heavy reliance on labor-intensive products and move toward products with more value and more advanced technology. China's active trade promotion policy has achieved obvious results.

China has made more progress in economic modernization than in political reform. The ultimate success of China's comprehensive reform, however, will depend on political reform. Deng Xiaoping voiced the need to create sound political institutions as early as 1980. He stated, "If these [leadership] systems are sound, they can place restraints on the actions of bad people; if they are unsound, they may hamper the efforts of good people or indeed, in certain cases, may push them in the wrong directions."[12] However, the deep fear of any signs of instability prevented Deng from taking drastic moves in political reform. China continues to face daunting challenges of political reform. In August 2010, Premier Wen said, "If there is no guarantee of reform of the political system, then results obtained from the reform of the economic system may be lost, and the goal of modernization cannot be achieved."[13] Wen's speech caused a new round of debate on political reform among China's intellectuals. However, the official news media remained quiet for a while before claiming that the current policy did not need any fundamental adjustment. It seems that democratic political reform has not gained majority support among the top leaders. Over the long run, it is most likely that the growing popular demand for democracy will force the leadership to take action in that direction. If the leadership does not respond to popular demand, the regime's legitimacy might decline.

THE SOCIALIST MARKET ECONOMY

Prior to the reform, the market was considered a feature of capitalism, and the plan was deemed a core element of socialism. By 1978, Chinese reformers learned that the centrally planned economy had many fundamental weaknesses. The reform from the beginning was market oriented. But it was not until 1992 that the leadership fully embraced the market economy as a key feature of the Chinese economic system. Deng Xiaoping emphasized that China should build "socialism with Chinese characteristics." He considered China's characteristics to be its populousness and its poor economic foundation. A key way to change that weak foundation would be to move away from the centrally planned economy. Chinese reformers have realized that there is no viable alternative to building a market economy.[14] One of the most innovative reform policies was the establishment of

Night traffic in Shenzhen, one of China's rapidly growing urban centers. (Flat Earth.)

the special economic zones (SEZs) in Shenzhen, Zhuhai, Shantou, and Xiamen. The SEZs were allowed favorable policies for imports, exports, and foreign investment. In three decades, Shenzhen grew from a fishing village to a dynamic modern city with over 10 million people. The SEZs significantly promoted Chinese exports without threatening the domestic economy.

By the mid-1980s, building "socialism with Chinese characteristics" became the primary theme defining the CCP's task. There is no doubt that this view of socialism symbolizes a decisive shift from Maoist to modernization models.[15] Socialism with Chinese characteristics equals an economy moving rapidly and sometimes painfully from central planning to market-driven decision making. It is an economy with a shrinking state-owned sector, a small collective sector, and a rapidly burgeoning private sector.

The central government now controls just under half of the assets of the state-owned sector (the other half having been sold off in the form of shares of stock) and manages these enterprises under the State-Owned Assets Supervision and Administration Commission. The commission was set up in 2003 to consolidate the several ministries, each of which had been devoted to a single industrial sector.[16]

The private sector in China has grown with remarkable rapidity over the last 30 years. Today well more than half of China's GDP is produced by privately owned businesses, and those businesses employ some 200 million workers, about a quarter of the economy's total workforce. By 2007 the cumulative total of contracted foreign investment in China had reached $1.6 trillion, and goods produced by foreign-invested firms account for more than half of China's exports.[17] The annual FDI in China exceeded $100 billion for the first time in 2010.

Because China has been moving away from the centrally planned economy and has most actively embraced core features of the market economy, it might be appropriate to describe its current economic system as "capitalism with Chinese characteristics."[18] Domestic conditions and supportive policies are critical in the rapid rise of China as a trading power. The needed conditions and policies include comparative advantage; a high level of saving and investment; special economic zones and special policies favoring foreign trade; currency devaluation and export promotion incentives; abundant supplies of labor with reasonable technical training and strong discipline; a supportive administrative and political framework for foreign trade; an emerging legal system promoting and protecting foreign trade; and strong local initiatives and central promotion. The global context since the end of the 1970s has been mostly in favor of China's reform and opening to the outside world. How long that benign global context can last remains to be seen. Regardless of that time period, China's rise as a trading power has profound strategic implications for building a secure and prosperous world.

At the 14th CCP Congress in 1992, the reform leaders ratified the need to shift China from being a "socialist planned commodity economy" to being a "socialist market economy." This change in terminology was extremely important, insofar as it legitimated the abolition of traditional mechanisms of central planning in favor of the introduction of macroeconomically regulated market competition. In the absence of direct state planning, the "socialist" component of the socialist market economy would henceforth be limited almost exclusively to public ownership of productive property.[19] This ideological change has enabled many policy innovations necessary for building a market economy. The command economy is dead. China today has a dynamic emerging market economy. With the exception of very few items, the price of goods in the Chinese market is decided by supply and demand. Consumers and producers both rely on and respond to the market. As a result, productivity and efficiency have risen significantly in the Chinese economy. At the same time, many problems associated with the emerging market economy, such as inequality, have also developed in China.

GROWING GAP BETWEEN THE RICH AND POOR

Prior to market reforms, China had a distinctive pattern of inequality because of a rural-urban divide that essentially created two forms of socialism within one country. In towns and cities, the socialist revolution created historically unprecedented security as well as an industrial working class whose standard of living approached that of managers and professionals. During the 1970s, average city incomes were triple those in the countryside, and urban income inequality was one of the lowest in the world. Rural residents, however, gained meager rewards from the socialist revolution. The collectivization of rural land in the early 1950s had reduced within-village inequalities. But inequalities between villages were significant.[20]

In contrast to the dramatic success of industrial modernization, China's agricultural sector has lagged behind. A central problem in this chapter is why agriculture boomed so vigorously in the 1980s only to go into the doldrums since the 1990s. The issues of peasants, agriculture, and the countryside have become key challenges affecting whether China can actually achieve modernity. The recent pursuit of the so-called socialist new countryside has been quite elusive, with many rural leaders continuing to focus on local industrialization instead of "agricultural modernization." Deng's policy of "allowing some people and some regions to become rich first" has led to severe disparity and gross inequality among Chinese regions and among different socioeconomic groups. After encouraging progress was made in the early 1980s, the urban-rural divide has only increased. Millions of rural Chinese are leaving their land and moving into cities. Discontent and social unrest are growing. Large-scale public disturbances have been on the rise in China for more than a decade. Such challenges have received scholarly attention in a growing body of literature on "rightful resistance." China has a long history of popular protest. Although reform and opening have lifted more than 600 million Chinese out of poverty, poverty and inequality are still major socioeconomic issues in China today. China now lacks a social safety net. "Harmonious society" is aimed at addressing growing disparity and popular discontent, but whether it can achieve its ambitious goals remains to be seen.

From 1988 to 1995, inequality of rural household per capita income rose an estimated 23 percent; urban inequality increased even faster—by 42 percent. Since the 1990s, both income gap and regional disparities have continued to increase. Seldom has the world witnessed so sharp and fast a rise in inequality as has occurred in China. Increasing economic and social inequality has therefore been an important subtext in the generally positive story of rapid growth accompanying economic reform and transition, and it calls into question the sustainability of that growth by raising the specter of social instability.[21] The ideology of egalitarianism sacrificed efficiency and incentives, and thus it led to a low efficiency level in the economy. The reformers have encouraged some people to become rich first. Such policies were designed to overcome egalitarianism in income distribution and promote efficiency with monetary incentives. Inequality of property income is a new problem. There was almost no property income for Chinese individuals in the prereform period, except for some interest earnings from bank savings deposits. Since the reform, however, property income of individuals, especially of urban residents, has increased rapidly, and its distribution is quite unequal.[22]

For many years, reformers promoted the idea that "getting rich is glorious" and encouraged some people and some regions to become rich first. Such policies naturally favored the people with better education and greater skills. The opening policy especially favored the coastal areas, with their good infrastructure and strong entrepreneurial tradition. Much rural poverty has been and still is concentrated in remote, ecologically disadvantaged areas of the northwest and southwest. The large net outflow of income from the poor to the state and collective, the declining educational attainment of the poor, and the sharply increasing costs they face for health care all cast spotlights on the fiscal decentralization of the reform era and the resulting heightened regressive burden on poor areas and poor people, perhaps especially in areas not targeted for poverty relief measures. Greater fiscal resources for the poor population, wherever they live, and sharply increased investment in public schooling and health care are needed core ingredients in a revitalized poverty reduction program for rural China.[23]

Growing inequality has led to more social resistance in China. More and more reformers realize that economic reform alone cannot solve the complex challenges of modernization. Now is the time for China to conduct comprehensive social reform in order to alleviate the pains of economic inequality. China urgently needs to develop more accessible health care, more affordable college education, and more reliable retirement systems. Social reforms, however, cannot be accomplished without political reforms. It is widely known that China's political reform lags behind its socioeconomic reform. Without meaningful political reform, China's economic development is not sustainable.

CHALLENGES OF URBANIZATION

Since the early 1980s, China has been undergoing rapid urbanization. The urban population has grown from less than 30 percent to close to half of the total population. About 70 percent of the rural workforce is employed in agriculture (including farming, forestry, fishing, and animal husbandry). There is a substantial surplus of labor in Chinese agriculture; some estimate that as many as 200 million rural workers could be redeployed with no reduction in agricultural output.[24] The remaining 594 million Chinese people are urban residents. About 294 million of them are in the workforce. In the prereform era, the majority of the urban workforce relied on the state to provide jobs. Under reform, the state sector is shrinking. The overwhelming majority of the urban workforce is employed in the nonstate sectors. However, there is very intense competition for government jobs, as more and more people search for stability and job security in this age of great transition and big uncertainties.

In recent years, China's urban population has been augmented by nearly 25 percent with the arrival of as many as 150 million migrant (or floating) workers. It is most likely that more than 300 million Chinese will move from the countryside to cities in the next two decades. The construction of urban infrastructure—roads, bridges, sewers, water supply systems, and the like—while extensive, still lags behind population growth. Urbanization is creating enormous investment opportunities in public utilities and infrastructure. By 2025, more than 70 percent of Chinese will live in cities with more than 1 million people. More than 40 billion square meters of floor space (equivalent to 10 New York Cities) will be needed over the next two decade in China.[25]

Paced by strong economic growth, China's leading cities are also evolving very fast. The urbanization that took almost a century in the West is occurring in a decade or two in China. In 1979, Shenzhen was still a poor fishing village with some 20,000 inhabitants. In 2009, it had a population of 9 million, and income per capita exceeded $13,600. Now Shenzhen plans to achieve an average GDP per capita of $20,000 by 2015. Yet, despite these colossal shifts, China's urbanization still has a long way to go. In 1980, the U.S. urban population was 74 percent of the total; China's comparable figure was only 19 percent. Today, America's urban share of the population is more than 80 percent, whereas China's remains less than 50 percent. Taking into consideration China's colossal size and development level, this gap suggests extraordinary potential. Very soon China will have 130 cities with more than 1 million people.[26] In fact, the preceding figures might very well be understating the pace and scope of China's urbanization. Such high-speed urbanization on an enormous scale has profound implications for both China and the outside world.

PROGRESS AND PROBLEMS IN HEALTH CARE

China had a very weak public health care system in the beginning of the People's Republic. From the 1950s to the 1970s, a comprehensive health care system was developed in the urban areas. In Chinese cities, a system of street clinics, district hospitals, and city hospitals was set up. In the countryside, there was the rural Cooperative Medical Scheme (CMS). Village clinics were staffed by "barefoot doctors" who received one year of training beyond junior high school. At the commune hospitals, doctors often had three years of medical training. The county hospitals were staffed with senior doctors who could provide care for more complicated cases. As a result of the broad access to public health care, China's public health made significant progress. Infant mortality was reduced, many infectious diseases were prevented and/or treated, and life expectancy was significantly raised from a very low level to a highly respectable level for a developing country.[27]

The barefoot doctor system was used during the time of the people's communes. But because of the household responsibility system and the end of the people's communes in the early 1980s, the barefoot doctor system no longer had the funding to continue. The failure of the cooperative health care system has had negative consequences on rural public health. With rising health care costs and vanished collective support, fewer and fewer peasants can afford to seek health care. Many people are afraid of seeking treatment. Because of the lack of timely treatment, many people's health has deteriorated. When patients do get treatment for serious diseases, the medical bills often get them deep into debt. Some people are driven into bankruptcy due to the mounting health care costs.

Health care cost has been rising faster than personal income. The Chinese population is slightly more than half rural. But the overwhelming majority of the doctors are in the cities, and good doctors especially tend to be concentrated in large urban centers. Even in the urban areas, many citizens can no longer afford health care because of the rising cost. It is widely believed that China's health care reform has been a failure.

As a result of the blind pursuit of profits and the lack of effective regulation and supervision, fake drugs and toxic food have caused severe negative consequences in China. One of the worst cases was the fake baby milk scandal that caused malnourishment among large number of children in 2004.[28] Many babies became seriously sick, and some even died of malnutrition after drinking milk with no nutritional value. In July 2007, authorities executed the former head of China's food and drug administration, as it was found that he had been accepting bribes in return for approving products, including medications, that were not safe. In 2008, the authorities arrested numerous people who had been selling melamine-tainted milk to dairy companies.[29]

In 2005, the New Rural Cooperative Medical Care System was introduced. Under this system, the annual cost of medical coverage is 50 yuan (about U.S. $7) per person. Of that, 20 yuan is paid by the central government, 20 yuan by the provincial government, and a contribution of 10 yuan is made by the patient. Medical coverage is also made available to most urban residents who were previously not covered. In the city of Kunming, for instance, an individual can buy a medical coverage plan for about 150 yuan (about U.S. $22). Although the total coverage remains at a low level, the increasing availability of health care plans has improved access to medical service. It is mostly likely that China's health care system will continue to improve with the overall rise of personal income and as a result of deeper reform in the health care system.

Rising health care costs and unequal distribution of health care resources are serious concerns for Chinese citizens. Many people are forced to save as much as 30 percent or even 40 percent of their income because of concerns for their health care, education, housing, and retirement. The extremely high level of saving has distorted China's economy and limited consumer spending. China must address health care, education, and housing issues in order to improve public health, achieve better economic balance, and enhance social harmony.

THE ENVIRONMENT AND SUSTAINABLE DEVELOPMENT

Rapid economic growth in China has come at a toll to both the local and global environment. China's environmental problems include poor water quality and water scarcity, air pollution in both urban and rural areas, land degradation, and increased desertification. These environmental challenges impact the health and welfare of the current population, threaten the prospects for future generations, and challenge China's ability to sustain economic growth rates in coming decades. China relies 70 percent on coal for its energy resources. Most sources of pollution in China can be traced back to energy use and particularly to reliance on coal.[30]

China is the largest consumer of energy with heavy reliance on coal in the world. Coal burning discharges sulfur dioxide and greenhouse gases into the air. China is a large contributor to global warming. Urban air pollution leads to many illnesses and adds up to huge health care costs. In 2007, Premier Wen Jiabao declared that global climate change is an undeniable fact. China must take active measures to fight against greenhouse emissions that contribute to global warming. At the UN conference on climate change in Copenhagen, Denmark, in December 2009, China declared that it is going to reduce its "carbon intensity"—a measure of carbon dioxide emissions per unit of GDP—by 40–45 percent by 2020, compared with 2005 levels.

Air pollution, water crisis, and other forms of environmental degradation have negatively affected the well-being of the Chinese people.

This photo, taken on June 13, 2003, shows a bird's-eye view of the Three Gorges Dam on the Chang Jiang (Yangtze River) in central China's Hubei Province. (AP Photo/Xinhua, Du Huaju.)

China's top officials and environmentalists have realized the heavy cost of GDP-focused growth patterns. The government is aware of the environmental problems and is working toward ways to address the environmental issues. Article 26 of the 1982 Constitution requires that "the state protects and improves the environment in which people live and the ecological environment. It prevents and controls pollution and other public hazards." China has passed several laws of environmental protection. However, enforcement of the laws has been relatively weak.

China's economic development strategy must focus more on being resource efficient and environmentally friendly. China has to import more than 40 percent of its oil, but its energy consumption per unit of GDP is 2.4 times higher than the world average. The government has called for a reorientation of the economic growth model toward sustainable growth with a lighter environmental impact. Environmental consciousness among the Chinese people is growing rapidly. There is growth demand for scientific development and greater focus on a green GDP.

Building a sustainable economy remains a most challenging task for the Chinese. To solve its energy and resource problems, China is increasingly turning to multinational development agencies and to foreign investment. China has also intensified its efforts in search of energy in Central Asia, Africa, and even Latin America. In a short period of time, China moved from being an oil exporter to being a net oil importer. In 2006, China for the first time became a coal importer. That is quite dramatic, because for a long time China had been the largest producer and a key exporter of coal. China's heavy reliance on coal and other fossil fuels has produced very negative results.[31] More and more Chinese have realized that China can no longer rely on energy-intensive growth. The national leadership has called for a fundamental shift toward "a new pattern of sustainable development." The state has significantly increased investment in renewable energy, including wind, solar, and hydroelectric power. In spite of such efforts, renewable energy only accounts for a small percentage of China's total energy consumption today.

Chapter 6

Law and Order

TENSIONS BETWEEN VIRTUE (*DE*) AND LAW (*FA*)

For more than 2,000 years, most traditional Chinese rulers emphasized what is called the "rule of man." Political guidelines of traditional China included elements of both *de* (virtue) and *fa* (law). Confucian scholars emphasized "rule by virtue" or moral force, while the legalists stressed "rule by law." Confucius stressed the role of ethics, morality, and education in good governance: if everyone would behave according to the proper rituals and ethical norms, society would be in harmony, and stability would be achieved. The ruler should be a father figure, providing a moral example for everyone. If all leaders would cultivate high morality and behave virtuously, peace and harmony could be realized. The legalists, in contrast, believed that human beings are basically selfish and should be governed by strict laws that would severely punish the lawbreakers. Laws in the legalist tradition reflected the wishes of the rulers. Law was perceived as an instrument for the ruler against the ruled. In that sense, China did not have a tradition similar to that of the "rule of law" as developed in the West.[1]

There are meaningful differences between rule by law and rule of law. Rule by law refers to effectively and consistently applying legal rules as a principal means for regulating economic, social, and political behavior. Rule of law goes beyond rule by law, in that the laws and legal system are a reliable constraint upon, and not merely a tool of, government. Rule of law requires some substantive standard of protecting human rights and citizens' liberties. China is still in the early stage of a long march toward the rule of law.

A Chinese scholar summarizes the characteristics of the Chinese traditional legal system in the following three aspects. First, it was a secular rather than a religious legal system. Chinese legal culture has traditionally been framed in terms of "ruler to the ruled" rather than in terms of "God to the people." Second, the ethical nature of traditional Chinese law was reflected in the three Confucian cardinal guidelines, namely "the ruler over the subject, the father over the son, and the husband over the wife." These ethical guidelines gradually became the key content of the legal system in Chinese feudal society. Third, emphasis was laid on the rule of man instead of the rule of law. Relating to this was the combination of administrative, legislative, and judicial authorities into one, with the emperor as the head of all three. The emperor was understood to have received instructions from heaven and was the highest legal authority.[2]

The long tradition of the rule of man hindered China's move toward legal rational authority. Revolutionary movements in 20th-century China destroyed traditional regimes. However, traditional authority patterns as embodied in old culture continue to affect people's thinking and behavior. In the 1950s, there were some efforts at building a legal system. Although the supremacy of the National People's Congress (NPC) was written into the first Constitution in 1954, in reality it was not realized because the Chinese Communist Party (CCP) dominated the Chinese political and legal system. Until the end of the 1970s, the NPC did not enact even one basic legal code. For example, there was no civil law, civil procedure law, criminal law, or criminal procedure law. Although the CCP destroyed the legal order created by the former Republic of China, it did not adopt a policy of building up a new legal system. The standards of state activities were based on the policies made by the CCP and on legal documents issued by the State Council or local governments. From the beginning of the 1950s to the beginning of the 1980s, the State Council issued more than 1,000 legal norms or documents, and most of them were not made in accordance with laws.[3] Most of the regulations issued by the State Council and local governments concerned the planned economy; therefore, they cannot be called laws in the modern sense.

Mao Zedong dominated Chinese politics from 1949 to 1976. He emphasized the key role of CCP leadership while downplaying the role of law. Mao believed in ideological principles, not laws. Ideological principles gave rise to a "line" of correct thinking, which in turn was translated into specific policies. He believed that it would be more convenient to rely on party policies than laws. It was in the Mao era that the arbitrary use of power by a few individuals and the supremacy of the party and administrative power were bred. In the 1957 antirightist campaign, many judges and lawyers were labeled as rightists and removed from their positions. In 1959, the Ministry of Justice and the Bureau of Legislative Affairs under the State Council were abolished. That action was then followed by the abolishment of the justice bureaus in every province, autonomous region, and municipality. When the Cultural Revolution started in 1966, Chinese society had been deprived of any functioning legal system. There was no legal control of acts that violated citizen rights. The rule of men was the norm in China before reform and opening began in the late 1970s.

The Cultural Revolution during 1966–1976 represented a period of lawlessness and chaos. Political disorder totally replaced the legal order. PRC president Liu Shaoqi was thrown into jail without any legal procedure. He died in prison under a stranger's name in 1969. The NPC was not able to take the responsibility to act as stipulated by the Constitution. From 1966 to 1975, the NPC could not hold the regular meetings accorded by the Constitution. This violated the Constitution, which specified that the NPC must hold a conference annually. All Chinese laws made before 1966 became empty words on paper. Aside from the radical Constitution of 1975, the state legislature did not make any law between 1966 and 1975.

At the 1997 CCP National Congress, General Secretary Jiang Zemin stated that "the development of democracy must be combined with the improvement of legal system so as to govern the country by law."[4] In 1999, rule of law was first endorsed by an amendment to the Constitution. Interestingly, after China had officially endorsed the concept of rule of law, Jiang Zemin put forward a new concept, rule by virtue, in 2001. He said, "In the governance of a country, rule of law and rule of virtue are always complementary to each other and mutually advanced. Neither is dispensable or abolishable."[5] Jiang acknowledged that his "virtue" was based on the ancient Chinese ethical tradition. It cannot be denied that rule by virtue carries strong rule of man characteristics, especially when it comprises traditional Chinese ethics and traditional CCP ethics. When rule by virtue is over-emphasized, rule of man will prevail again, which is the opposite of the rule of law. It can be seen from the rule by virtue doctrine that China is not yet ready for the genuine rule of law and has continued to use law as a ruling instrument.[6]

Although the debates about rule by virtue and rule of law remain intense in China today, there is no denial that the rule of law has been established as a core objective of China's modernization.[7] It is interesting that the first major study session of the Politburo under Hu Jintao was devoted to studying the Chinese Constitution. Constitutionalism is a key component of the rule of law.[8] In current Chinese politics, however, the party leadership continues to be the dominant feature. If any political party can act above the law, then the "rule of law" will be empty words. China's long history of the rule of man suggests that there is a long way to go before the rule of law can be fully put into practice. As China continues to modernize, the rule of law might gradually take root.

CRIME AND PUNISHMENT

Fighting against crime and maintaining social order are basic functions of good governance. Crime prevention in China is typically represented by the comprehensive treatment of public security problems. A main goal of the government is to maintain public order and reduce crime. Like all societies in rapid modernization, China has been confronting a growing number and variety of crimes in recent years. Crime prevention and law enforcement are among the most rapidly growing sections of China's state. In 2010, the Chinese government spent nearly as much money in maintaining domestic security as it spent on national defense, which is more than its health care budget.[9] In addition to large police and armed police forces, there are an estimated 5 million private security guards in China.

China's judicial system, which applies and enforces the law, comprises 3,631 people's courts at four levels corresponding to the political structure, with the Supreme People's Court (SPC) at the apex.[10] There are three levels of court systems below the SPC: (1) basic people's courts at the level of the counties, towns, and municipal districts; (2) intermediate people's courts at the level of prefectures and municipalities;

and (3) high people's courts at the level of provinces, autonomous regions, and centrally administered municipalities.

The available forms of legal punishment, as stipulated in the 1979 and 1997 Criminal Law codes, include control, short-term detention, fixed-term imprisonment, life imprisonment, and the death penalty. Supplementary punishments include fines, deprivation of political rights, and confiscation of property. As the least severe form of punishment, control is typically applied to first-time offenders and offenders who have committed minor offenses. Offenders are placed in the community under surveillance while being allowed to engage in routine activity such as living with family and going to work. Prisons are typically located in remote areas. It is believed that labor is instrumental and critical in altering one's mind-set and habits. Labor keeps inmates busy and helps them develop good work habits and cooperative spirits, master essential vocational skills, and cultivate their minds.

The death penalty is reserved for offenders who have committed the most serious and dangerous crimes. The 1997 Criminal Law stipulates 68 offense types that are subject to the death penalty. In 2007 the SPC reinstated its authority to review all capital sentences, an authority that had been delegated to provincial courts in 1983 in order to counter the mounting wave of crimes in the country. The number of executions dropped significantly after 2007. The number of crimes for which the death penalty is appropriate will be significantly limited in the future. The death sentence cannot be applied to individuals under 18 years old or to pregnant women. In recent years, there has been more strict limitation of applying the death penalty. At the same time, there is growing discussion about the possible abolishment of the death penalty. In light of the global trend to abolish or strictly limit the application of capital punishment, some Chinese scholars are rethinking the legislative basis for the death penalty and China's current excessive confidence in and reliance on it. Despite the impossibility of completely abolishing the death penalty in China today, considering its defects, the existing policy of "less and cautious application of the death penalty, and criminals who may be sentenced to death or not shall not be sentenced to death" should be strictly implemented. At the present stage, the abolition of the death penalty for economic crimes should be placed first on the agenda.[11] The majority view in China, however, remains that the death penalty should be kept as deterrence against and punishment for the most vicious crimes.

Since the 1980s, the CCP Central Commission of Politics and Law has launched "strike-hard" campaigns from time to time. Such campaigns usually focused on three kinds of crimes: (1) crimes committed by Mafia-style gangs and other organized criminal groups; (2) serious violent crimes including bombings, willful murder, armed robbery, and kidnapping; and (3) crimes such as burglary, theft, and other offenses that pose a serious threat to social order and security. During the campaigns, the courts had to follow CCP instructions and work in cooperation with other criminal justice organs to punish the criminals identified.[12] Each wave of strike-hard campaigns focused on different types of crimes, depending on the pressing social issues of the time. The common objectives of strike-hard campaigns were to suppress criminal elements through swift and severe enforcement of law and punishment. In 2003, for instance, the campaigns focused on violent crime, property offenses, organized crime, economic and corruption offenses, narcotics offenses, sex offenses, and gambling. Crime prevention has increasingly met challenges since the 1980s because of the changing political and socioeconomic structure of China. Economic development has precipitated a host of changes in interpersonal relationships, rights consciousness, social control, and opportunities for crime. Crime rates have skyrocketed in the past three decades, particularly in the areas of prostitution, drug trafficking, organized crime, and corruption.

In recent years, China has witnessed multiple violent attacks against children in elementary schools. Such violent crimes have heightened social tension and created widespread fear for personal safety. Chongqing party secretary Bo Xilai took decisive action against criminal groups with close connections to some senior city officials and dozens of police officers. As a result of the campaign, the former head of Chongqing's judiciary department, Wen Qiang, was sentenced to death in 2010 for charges including rape, bribery, and protecting an underground criminal gang. The campaign also resulted in more than 3,000 detentions and hundreds of prosecutions.[13] Such campaigns against organized crime are very popular but have caused concern among some legal scholars. Some scholars are afraid that politicians might overstep legal boundaries through taking popular anticrime actions. Many of China's reformers prefer to strengthen the rule of law against crime rather than relying on a few strong-man politicians to maintain order. If a government has to rely on a strong man, who is going to make sure that the strong man will not become corrupt? Over the long term, only the rule of law can provide effective answers to such critical questions.

A LONG MARCH TOWARD THE RULE OF LAW

From the founding of the PRC in 1949 until 1953, the priority was to establish a new political and socioeconomic system. The new government abolished all the laws enacted under the previous government, and it did not immediately establish new codes to replace the old ones. The CCP relied on issuing policies as the basis for the administration of justice. In 1954, the first Constitution was approved. The government also later enacted the Organic Law of the People's Courts and the Organic Law of the People's Procuratorates. However, Mao Zedong continued to favor the rule of party policy over that of law. During the Cultural Revolution, China's legal system was almost totally replaced by "feudalist-fascist dictatorship" (as post-Mao official language described the violent period).

The political chaos, social turmoil, mass terror, and economic breakdown of the Cultural Revolution (1966–1976) caused many Chinese to rethink the proper role of law and the need for political reform. The Chinese debate over the rule of law in the late 1970s and 1980s originated in the far-reaching political reaction to the Cultural Revolution. The policy to create a "rule-of-law state" started to take shape in December 1978, when the CCP leadership decided to end mass class struggle and shift to modernization. The CCP communiqué stated:

In order to safeguard the people's democracy, it is imperative to strengthen the social legal system so that democracy is systematized and written into law in such a way as to ensure the stability, continuity, and full authority of this democratic system and laws; there must be laws for people to follow, these laws must be observed, and their enforcement must be strict and lawbreakers must be dealt with.[14]

The communiqué called upon judicial and prosecutorial personnel to maintain their independence and to guarantee the equality of all people before the law, denying anyone the privilege of being above the law.

Deng Xiaoping was twice a victim of political persecution without any legal process. Deng envisioned a

> government of law, not men. Democracy has to be institutional-ized and written into law, so as to make sure that institutions and laws do not change whenever the leadership changes or whenever the leaders change their views. The trouble now is that our legal system is incomplete. Very often what leaders say is taken as law and anyone who disagrees is called a lawbreaker. That kind of law changes whenever leaders' views change. So we must concentrate on enacting criminal and civil codes, procedural laws, and other necessary laws. These laws should be discussed and adopted through democratic procedures.[15]

Following the CCP decision to modernize the economy and build up the socialist legal system, the Constitution was changed in 1982. The PRC's first Constitution came into being in 1954. The second and third were drawn up in 1975 and 1978. The 1982 Constitution (which has been amended) is the one still in force today. The 1982 Constitution stipulates that the NPC is the supreme organ of state power, and it also describes the supremacy of the Constitution and laws—namely, that no state organs, political parties, organizations, enterprises, or individuals are allowed to violate the Constitution and laws. As the preamble to the Constitution also stipulates that the CCP has to take responsibility for the leadership of the country, however, this gives the CCP a legal potential to act above all other organs of power.

China has made some progress in its struggle for the rule of law. In 1979, the NPC adopted the PRC's first code of criminal law and crimi-nal procedure law. It also adopted the Organic Law of the People's Courts of the People's Republic of China (1980) and the Organic Law of the People's Procuratorates of the People's Republic of China (1980). A system of administration according to law is being estab-lished. The Administrative Litigation Law was adopted and went into effect in 1991. It is the first law in Chinese history to protect citizens' rights to bring public officials to court through formal legal procedures. The State Compensation Law, the Administrative Review Law, the

Administrative Punishment Law, and other related laws were adopted and implemented thereafter. China has sped up the process of legislation on economic laws during the transition to the market economy. Through three decades of effort, a new legal system has been formulated. The new laws include administrative law, civil law, economic law, marriage law, labor law, social welfare law, law for the protection of natural resources and environment, criminal law, procedure law, and military law. From 1979 to 1999, the NPC and its Standing Committee passed more than 250 laws and more than 100 legal decisions; the State Council issued more than 830 executive legal regulations, and local people's congresses made more than 6,000 local laws and regulations.[16] Social and economic conflicts, which had been handled by administrative methods in the past, are now often handled through law and the judicial process.

The 15th CCP National Congress, held in 1997, adopted "rule according to law." In 1999, the NPC amended the 1982 Constitution to stress ruling the country in accordance with the law. The amended Constitution states, "The People's Republic of China practices ruling the country in accordance with the law and building a socialist country of law." In 2004, new amendments to the Constitution emphasize protecting private property and human rights. "The State protects the lawful rights and interests of the non-public sectors of the economy such as the individual and private sectors of the economy." "Citizens' lawful private property is inviolable." "The State respects and preserves human rights." The rule of law, if successfully established and implemented, will provide a solid foundation for China's development of democracy and the market economy. China has worked hard over the last three decades to become a society governed by laws rather than by individuals.[17]

Over the past decade, China has experienced a marked increase in unrest. According to official statistics, the number of mass incidents increased from 8,700 in 1993 to 40,000 in 2002, 58,000 in 2003, and 74,000 in 2004. The number of protesters involved reportedly increased from 860,000 in 1993 to 3.7 million in 2004.[18] Disgruntled villagers deprived of land with meager compensation, migrant workers petitioning for back pay, laid-off workers at state-owned enterprises, and well-organized demobilized soldiers demanding welfare payments were believed to be the main groups behind these mass incidents.[19]

If serious and timely measures are not taken, such growing unrest and social resistance will endanger the survival of the Chinese state.[20] Solving such tough problems requires citizen empowerment and state capacity. If the central government is not able to enforce laws protecting citizens' rights, citizens have to stand up to defend their own rights. The Chinese state must strengthen its capacity for protecting civil rights. A combination of rights consciousness from below and political promotion of rights from above will serve the advancement of Chinese political modernization. Merle Goldman stated:

> Democracy depends on the desire of organized citizens to participate in the political process in order to hold the political authority accountable for its actions and to improve the public good. There can be citizenship without democracy, but there cannot be democracy without citizen participation.[21]

In the last three decades, China has done a remarkable job of creating a fairly complete system of substantial law. In 2004, the policy on "Implementing Administration in Accordance with Law" officially ushered in a new era of law-based government in China. As of 2009, China counted 231 laws, some 600 administrative regulations, and 7,000 local rules and regulations currently in force. China also has about 600 regulations issued by the autonomous regions of China and numerous departmental rules at all levels that regulate different aspects of daily life. In 1978, fewer than 2,000 lawyers could be identified. By 2008, however, China had more than 600 institutions of higher learning offering bachelors' degrees in law, nearly 157,000 licensed lawyers, and over 14,000 law firms.[22] Despite the sobering limitations on the role of the courts and the legal profession in helping realize the rule of law in China, these two institutions are in fact playing an ever greater role within Chinese society.

CORRUPTION AND LEGITIMACY CRISIS

Post-Mao China has experienced unprecedented levels of corruption. Numerous public opinion surveys since the late 1980s have shown corruption to be the top concern among the general public. Corruption is likely to occur under two sets of circumstances. One is the presence of opportunity, such as the extensive role of the government as a regulator, allocator, producer, and employer; the weakening of institutional and legal sanctions; and the prevalence of regulatory loopholes and legal ambiguities. The other is the presence of motivation, such as confusion over changing values; weakness of moral sanctions; relative impoverishment; and a lack of alternative access to self-enrichment.[23] Both circumstances exist in China's transition to the market.

Two aspects of Chinese society today combine to create a climate particularly conducive to corruption, and corruption that has become ubiquitous serves to undermine the legitimacy of both party and government, defying efforts to eliminate or at least to curb it. The first aspect is a mind-set inherited from the Confucian tradition and its emphasis on understanding society as a web of mostly hierarchical relationships. The line between the legitimate cultivation of reciprocal friendship and the corrupt practice of bribery is difficult to draw. Another element of Chinese society that is conducive to the growth of corruption is the economy's current state of incomplete marketization. Most decisions about allocating resources are made by the market, but decisions about allocating certain critical resources are still made by party and state officials. The sharp competition among the state, the collective, and the private sector has raised the ante in decisions about who gets what quantity of critical items in short supply, a situation rife with opportunities for corruption.[24]

Corruption is intractable because the legal system is not able to establish a standard against which to measure it, and the political system lacks an independent agency to attack and control it. Central authorities launch periodic anticorruption campaigns, but the agents on whom they rely to implement these campaigns are the very officials who are their most eligible targets. At best, a few scapegoats are prosecuted and lose their jobs, but the problem grows worse.[25] Two principle sources of corruption are greed coupled with abundant opportunities for profit raking and a weak legal environment replete with outdated rules and regulations. From 1999 to 2002, more than 1.5 million CCP members, including some officials, were investigated, sentenced, fined, or jailed. In 2002, Hu Changqing, who was the vice governor of Jiangxi Province, was sentenced to death and executed. The Yuanhua smuggling case in Fujian Province caught the attention of the central government, which had to send several thousand people to investigate and completely destroy the network that the Yuanhua company had operated for years.

Some scholars suggest that endemic corruption is inherent to authoritarian rule and thus continues to fester in the absence of political regime change. It can be argued, however, that the introduction of numerous institutional reforms that bear on corruption prevention, together with greater efforts to crack down on corruption, have allowed the Chinese leadership to make some initial progress in containing its spread. It is likely that further progress will be made to curb corruption and improve governance. Comprehensive initiatives to alter the institutional incentives for officials include: (1) completion of market transitions, (2) public sector management reforms, (3) greater political accountability, (4) stricter institutional restraints, and (5) more international norms and obligations.[26]

There are several trends in corruption in China. The first trend is cash corruption changing to capital corruption. Under the preform economic system dominated by public ownership, there was little chance of transferring state property into private ownership. While taking public funds was difficult, corrupt officials consumed them to satisfy their avarice. Cash corruption was common in the early stage of reform. As the scope of reform broadened, many officials began to engage in capital corruption, by transferring state assets into private hands. Such capital corruption surges in the process of transferring the bulk of state-owned enterprises into shareholding companies, where corrupt officials use different methods to get more individual shares or increase the value of the shares they control. Corruption may take place in land bidding processes as well, since local officials can disclose critical information to the party in their favor or set preferential bidding procedures for that party. For farmers, there is nothing worse than losing their land. Because of the skyrocketing profits of land speculation in Chinese urbanization and industrialization, many local officials are eager to engage in land corruption. The corrupt officials try to get as much land as possible from farmers at the lowest prices possible. Forced land enclosures by local governments have often led to widespread popular resistance. Many local governments have resorted to the use of force in the process of land corruption.[27]

The second trend is individual corruption changing to collective corruption. As China's reform spreads to various new economic areas, corruption is growing in complicity and sophistication. Corruption has evolved into a network of interactions involving exchanges and tradeoffs among a group of corrupt people who seek to maximize individual interests and minimize potential risks. Examples of collective corruption include organized smuggling, collective embezzlement, the receiving of bribes by a group of officials, and group consumption such as lavish banquets, extravagant office equipment, and public-funded sightseeing trips.[28]

The third alarming trend in China's corruption is that corruption is becoming increasingly transnational, as many corrupt activities are collaborative operations of domestic government officials with overseas individuals or organizations. As overseas business connections expand, smuggling has experienced quantitative and qualitative changes and become an important profiteering enterprise in recent years. The Yuanhua scandal, which smuggled a total of over 53 billion yuan–worth of scarce goods and production materials and evaded some 30 billion yuan in taxes, was first revealed in its deals with a U.S.-based shipping company to smuggle vegetable oil. The chief operator of the Yuanhua scandal, Lai Changxing, originally a farmer in China, began his business in Hong Kong as a mainland immigrant. Through bribery and other networking tactics, Lai soon became a good friend of many government officials in Xiamen after he returned from Hong Kong. His smuggling operations were assisted by several hundred officials, including a vice minister of public security in Beijing, two deputy mayors of Xiamen, and the director of the city's customs.[29] Lai Changxing escaped to Canada when the Chinese authorities took action against Yuanhua. The Chinese government has asked Canada to extradite him to China for trial. So far he has been able to avoid extradition through legal maneuvers.

Rampant corruption has caused public cynicism and disillusionment. It has threatened the legitimacy of the party-state. Of all the potential risks for instability that dot China's changing political landscape, none may be more lethal than corruption by government officials. The abuse of power for personal gain permeates nearly all layers and departments of government. Politically, corruption by members of the ruling elite undermines the legitimacy of the CCP, erodes the authority of the state, impedes the effective implementation of government policies, and fuels public resentment against the government. Economically, corruption creates distortion, increases the costs of commerce, causes waste and inefficiency, and stunts growth and employment. Socially, corruption exacerbates inequality, harms public safety, victimizes the poor and the powerless, and increases social injustice.[30] Indeed, corruption is a life and death issue for the Chinese leadership. The final solution to this critical issue will rely on building rule of law. Without an effective political and legal system, even good officials will become corrupt. With a democratic political system based on rule of law, all officials, especially the bad ones, will be under strict restrictions and will not be able to escape punishment for their wrongdoing.

OBSTACLES TO ESTABLISHING THE RULE OF LAW

China's judicial system was not intended to serve as a check and balance on the bureaucracy or legislation, nor does it so function. Its principal purpose is to serve as part of the apparatus of social control, alongside the police and the prosecutors' offices. Verdicts are subject to review and modification by senior party leaders at each level. They are also subject to appeal, and the Supreme People's Court (along with the CCP Politburo, which oversees its work) is the final court of appeal. The court cannot serve as a check on the work of the government, the legislature, or, least of all, the party. The court system's principal function is, rather, to apply policies, laws, and regulations to specific cases. China is in a transitional period in which the combination of "rule of man," "rule by law," and "rule of law" coexist. The current legal reform in China can be characterized as "rule of the party by law." It is not appropriate to use the standards of a mature legalized society to measure China's legal development.[31]

The development of economic law in China had a slow start, because the planned economy was based on administrative command rather than legislation to resolve disputes. Even in the age of economic reform, legalization turned out to be more challenging than expected. The Property Law was not passed until 2007. Another important item of legislation that was delayed for years was the Antimonopoly Law (2008). China's legal institutions are still weak by developed-country standards. It can take years to evolve into a society with efficient and qualified institutions and parties. It also takes time to change the general culture of institutions.[32]

It is very difficult to establish judicial independence in China, because all critical judicial appointments must be approved by the organizational department of the CCP. When the judges' professional careers are so totally dependent on party control, it is almost impossible for them to defend judicial independence. Furthermore, local governments control the finances of courts in their localities. As a result, many judges have to show deference to local party and government leaders. In recent years, many Chinese courts have experienced difficulty in enforcing their rulings. Enforcement is particularly weak if the losing side involved in the disputes does not reside in the administrative area of the court issuing the ruling.

A major objective of China's legal development project during the reform era has been to use law to control and constrain agents of the party and state. This agenda does not show a deep commitment to the rule of law. It may reflect a sense of the law's usefulness in pursuing the regime's self-interest in a more effective, disciplined, and legitimate party and state apparatus. That does not mean that the law reform is insignificant. Indeed, law often fares best when proponents see it as a means, not as an end in itself. China's leaders have come to appreciate that law can help address corruption, parochialism (including local protectionism), incompetence, excessive rent seeking, and abuse of power.[33]

The paradox is that the CCP continues to espouse a rule of law that also constrains state power while insisting on the primacy of the party. The tension between promotion of greater rule of law and one-party rule permeates the entire legal system. Nevertheless, the official rhetoric of legality and positive development of law and the legal institutions and processes are fostering a new culture of legality in the public and the party-state. These developments suggest that an increasingly transparent, participatory, and accountable China may well progress further along the continuum toward rule of law.[34] Over the long run, the rule of law and democratization must go hand-in-hand. Without democratic elections providing legitimacy for the political leadership and effective check of power at the top, the rule of law will not be able to take root. Democratization, however, cannot be achieved overnight. It will take much hard work over a long period of time to make democracy real.

Chapter 7

China's Place in a Changing World

DOMESTIC POLITICS AND FOREIGN RELATIONS

China is the most populous country in the world, with a glorious ancient civilization.[1] Since 1978, the Chinese economy has been growing at close to 10 percent a year. In 2010, China's gross domestic product (GDP) was valued at $5.87 trillion, surpassed Japan's $5.47 trillion, and became the world's second-largest economy after the United States. At the same time, Chinese politics are in transition. It is fitting to examine the connections between Chinese domestic politics and foreign relations. From 1949 to 1976, the People's Republic of China (PRC) experienced many political campaigns and dramatic socioeconomic transformations. In the era of reform and opening, China's top priority has been socioeconomic modernization. An interesting question is whether China's domestic politics are driving its foreign policy or the international circumstances are driving Chinese politics. It is reasonable to argue that China's internal development takes a higher priority than foreign relations for the Chinese leadership.

After more than six decades of economic development and political change, the PRC has emerged as one of the most dynamic economic powers with a distinctive political system in the world. China is becoming a world power that commands growing respect around the world.[2] At the same time, there is still much confusion and concern regarding China's intentions and ambitions among its neighbors and other world powers. There are contending perspectives on the so-called China threat.[3]

Some Chinese scholars and leaders have advocated a "peaceful rise" or "peaceful development." Such terms highlight the connections between China's domestic development and foreign relations. During 2003–2004, the Chinese leadership seriously discussed the term "peaceful rise" and then decided to use "peaceful development." This peaceful approach is deeply rooted in Chinese cultural tradition, socioeconomic development, and strategic choice. The Chinese classical educator and thinker Confucius strongly promoted civility, harmony, and humanity. Chinese cultural tradition, featuring "unity in diversity" and "priority to peace," goes a long way toward facilitating China's harmonious coexistence and sharing of prosperity with the Asia-Pacific region and the world at large.

When President Hu Jintao gave a keynote speech at the Boao Forum in 2004, he stressed peaceful development. Since then, "peaceful development" has been the official slogan, while scholars continue to debate both the concepts of peaceful rise and peaceful development. State Councillor Dai Bingguo, who is in charge of foreign affairs, reaffirms the path of peaceful development as long-term strategy that will last over 100 years. China will remain a developing country for a long time and will not challenge U.S. global leadership.[4]

Peaceful development is a strategic choice that was made by the Chinese leadership in the early 1980s. Deng Xiaoping clearly realized the critical link between peace and development. The transition from Mao Zedong's revolutionary diplomacy to Deng's pragmatic diplomacy was driven by the demands of the "four modernizations" of agriculture, industry, science and technology, and national defense. This shift reflects a fundamental transition from dogmatic and ideological foreign policy to a pragmatic policy based on China's national interests. One of Deng's basic assumptions is that there would be no world war in the foreseeable future. Therefore, China could concentrate on building its own economy and enhancing people's living standards. Another critical element of China's grand strategy is to achieve common development with neighboring countries. This good-neighbor policy has achieved remarkable results. In fact, the PRC today has better relations with almost all neighboring countries than at any time in its history. Deng publicly proclaimed that ideology should not affect diplomatic relations. Under the new strategy, Beijing does not decide friends or foes based on ideological considerations. The starting point of Chinese foreign policy is national interest.

China's current leadership continues to put domestic priority ahead of foreign relations. Diplomacy is to serve the goal of building a peaceful international environment for domestic development. In recent years, there have been significant debates about the rise of China and its implications for international relations. One of the key issues is whether China's rapid rise will be peaceful or disruptive to the existing international order. China's deep reform, that is, its profound political and socioeconomic change, requires a peaceful international environment, while a largely peaceful environment has contributed to China's successful economic reform. However, without meaningful political reform, China's growth may not be sustainable. When socioeconomic development runs into deep trouble, China might not be able to maintain its peaceful orientation in foreign policy. Thus, the relationship between peaceful development and China's reform is interdependent. Success in one will strengthen the other. On the other hand, failure or crisis in one aspect will certainly have negative consequences on the other. It seems that China's domestic politics are driving its foreign policy. Foreign policy, in turn, will have significant impact on China's domestic development. The connections between the two sides are truly complex and dynamic. Ultimately, it seems that domestic development is driving China's grand strategy. If China can successfully resolve its problems of economic development, social reform, and political restructuring, most of its foreign policy problems might also be easier to resolve.[5]

CHARACTERISTICS OF PEACEFUL DEVELOPMENT

A peaceful international environment is essential for achieving socioeconomic modernization. In a highly centralized political system, domestic factors, including elite politics, tend to play a more significant role in foreign policy than in a pluralist system. In the era of Mao Zedong, Mao himself played a dominant role in China's key foreign policy decisions. One of Mao's key assumptions in the 1960s and early 1970s was that war was inevitable and China must be prepared against it. In contrast, Deng Xiaoping's most significant policy was "to take economic development as the central task." Soon after Deng emerged as China's paramount leader in 1978, he made a fundamentally different assumption: that a world war would not break out in the foreseeable future. Thus, the core task should shift to building a modern economy. Since then, economic development has been a core objective for the Chinese leadership. Deng Xiaoping proposed the "independent peaceful foreign policy" in the early 1980s. China's most fundamental policy since the Deng era has been "reform and opening," aimed at building a strong and prosperous country. Foreign trade and foreign investment have played very important roles in China's economic development. China's dynamic and fruitful participation in the world economy is the result of peaceful and relatively stable global trading and financial systems. Foreign trade and foreign direct investment (FDI) will both be disrupted or even completely stopped if major armed conflict involving China occurs. China's remarkable achievements in promoting foreign trade and attracting FDI have vindicated the correctness of its emphasis on peaceful development.

In pursuit of its economic goals, China has improved relations with the broadest possible range of countries. Ideological obstacles to better relations were largely eliminated, and a pragmatic approach helped to resolve numerous problems with foreign powers. China has truly

This May 6, 2010, file photo shows a visitor standing next to the United Kingdom Pavilion at the World Expo in Shanghai, China. (AP Photo/Eugene Hoshiko, file.)

enjoyed the benefit of dynamic growth in a peaceful environment for three decades. In 2010 China overtook Japan as the second-largest economy in the world, only behind the United States.

There are numerous domestic and international challenges to China's peaceful development. It is beyond dispute that China has enjoyed an extraordinarily high growth rate for three decades. A key question is whether China's strong growth is sustainable. China faces multiple challenges to its development. The first is that of natural resources. Currently, China's exploitable oil and natural gas reserves, water resources, and arable land are all well below world average in per capita terms. With rapid economic growth, China's demand for energy and other resources is growing at unprecedented rates. The current pattern of extensive growth is not sustainable. The leadership has realized that China must find more alternative energy with a focus on renewable energy.

The second challenge is the environment. Serious pollution, the wasteful use of resources, and low rates of recycling are bottlenecks for sustainable economic development. China has become the largest producer and market for new cars. The demand for cars is growing very rapidly. Traffic jams in cities and air pollution are becoming more and more serious. Environmental degradation has not only heavy economic costs but also very negative consequences on human development. No economic growth can make up for the serious deterioration of people's health.

The third challenge is the lack of coordination between economic and social development. As the economy grows, socioeconomic inequality and regional disparities become more severe. Inflation is on the rise. Social tensions are growing in spite of the repeated calls for building a "harmonious society." As a developing country, China's social security system, health care system, and education system are relatively backward. Many citizens do not have a reliable safety net. Single-minded pursuit of GDP growth by many local leaders has led to unbalanced growth and rising social tensions. It seems that China's reform has come to a crossroads. The past path of "GDP growth as a priority" is turning into a dead end. Now is the time to seriously address comprehensive reforms, including social reform and political restructuring.

China has followed a good-neighbor policy and built friendly relations with almost all of its neighbors. The only major neighboring country

Fireworks explode over the National Stadium, known as the Bird's Nest, during the opening ceremony of the 2008 Summer Olympic Games in Beijing August 8, 2008. (AP Photo/Greg Baker.)

that has serious political differences with China is Japan. Tensions between the two countries were highlighted when Japan arrested a Chinese fishing boat captain near the disputed Diaoyu Islands (Senkaku Islands in Japanese) in the summer of 2010. Nationalism is also growing in China. It remains to be seen whether China and Japan can avoid the pitfalls of nationalist emotions to build their common interests. China is surrounded by a number of countries with troubled bilateral or multi-lateral relations. For instance, India and Pakistan have long been in territorial and religious disputes. The fact that both India and Pakistan are armed with nuclear weapons now makes the situation more intense. Premier Wen Jiabao visited India and Pakistan in December 2010, trying to promote friendly relations with both neighbors.

Beijing has serious concerns about security on the Korean Peninsula. North Korea has been developing a nuclear program. A nuclear North Korea will seriously disrupt the regional security order and have negative consequences for Beijing's peaceful foreign policy. Tensions on the Korean Peninsula reached a new dangerous level when South Korea claimed that its navy ship *Cheonan* was destroyed in a torpedo attack by a North Korean submarine in April 2010. In November 2010 North Korea shelled South Korea's Yeonpyeong Island, killing two South Korean marines and injuring more than a dozen people. South Korea returned fire. Both sides claimed that the other side fired first. China has called for a resumption of the Six Party Talks to resolve the North Korean nuclear crisis. It seems that diplomacy is the only viable approach to solve the crisis. The road to a satisfactory solution for all parties, however, is full of obstacles.

China and Russia are enjoying their best relations in decades. However, there is no certainty that Sino-Russian relations will always remain stable. In fact, both sides have some deeply rooted mistrust and mutual suspicion. Russia is also concerned with China's rapid economic growth and the potential growth of Chinese immigration to the Russian Far East. Nevertheless, it seems that common interests between Russia and China exceed their differences. China and Russia have conducted several rounds of joint military exercises since 2005. The two countries share some strategic concerns, especially on the common fight against terrorism, Islamic fundamentalism, and separatism in Chechnya and Taiwan. China and Russia have also increased their cooperation in energy, other resources, and technology. It is interesting that the official relations between Beijing and Moscow are very good, but people-to-people exchanges between citizens are less than ideal.

RELATIONS WITH THE UNITED STATES

China's relationship with the United States has special significance for China's domestic politics and foreign relations. China is the largest developing country, while the United States is the largest developed country. The relationship between the two countries has significant impact on global politics and economics. The most important bilateral relationship for China is Sino-American relations. A healthy relationship with the United States is critical for creating a favorable international environment for reform and opening, as well as for achieving China's modernization with the assistance of U.S. capital, technology, and management experience. The Cold War once separated China and the United States. It was mutual agreement on the common threat from the former Soviet Union that brought Beijing and Washington together in the 1970s. After the end of the Cold War and the disintegration of the Soviet Union, geoeconomics became more prominent than geopolitics in U.S.-China relations. With increasingly broad and active economic interaction between the two countries, it seems that U.S.-China cooperation is growing, but friction and misperceptions are rising as well. The Taiwan situation has been a critical issue in relations between Beijing and Washington. That issue is becoming increasingly interesting, due not only to changing perceptions in the two capitals but also to rapid development inside Taiwan, following the 2008 power transition from the proindependence Democratic Progressive Party to the pro–status quo Nationalist Party. Sino-American relations have evolved from a "fragile relationship" to a truly interdependent "complex relationship" to now a "positive, cooperative, and comprehensive relationship."

Reformers in China for a long time have looked to the United States as a leading modern country. Chinese leaders from Sun Yat-sen to Deng Xiaoping and Hu Jintao have held high regard for American efficiency. International circumstances, however, were not favorable for the United States to play an active role in Chinese modernization before the 1970s. In fact, the two countries were strategic rivals for more than two decades before the 1972 rapprochement. The rising Cold War confrontation between the United States and the Soviet Union and China's civil wars in the late 1940s made it impossible for China to develop a normal relationship with the United States in the beginning of the PRC.

Following the founding of the PRC in 1949, Mao Zedong decided to "lean to one side," relying on the Soviet Union. The outbreak of the Korean War in 1950 and the Chinese "anti-American and assist-Korea" campaign deepened the Cold War confrontation between the two sides. In addition to fighting against Chinese forces in the Korean

Peninsula, the United States deployed its Seventh Fleet in the Taiwan Strait, effectively blocking the mainland from taking over Taiwan. Mao perceived the United States as the biggest threat to China's national security in the 1950s and early 1960s.

Ideological differences and conflicts of national interest between Beijing and Moscow grew more serious in the late 1950s and led to open debates in the early 1960s. In 1969, China and the Soviet Union engaged in armed border clashes. Confronted with the rising Soviet challenge, Mao Zedong decided to improve relations with the United States. From the U.S. side, President Richard Nixon and his national security adviser Henry A. Kissinger also took bold initiatives to open up to China. It was a common strategic consideration against the growing Soviet threat that brought Beijing and Washington together. In February 1972, President Nixon visited China. Nixon's meeting with Chairman Mao and the Shanghai Communiqué issued by the two governments helped to build a strategic foundation for developing Sino-American relations. For several years, China and the United States were unable to fully normalize diplomatic relations because of their differences on the issue of Taiwan.

Mao Zedong died in September 1976. The next Chinese paramount leader, Deng Xiaoping, saw the establishment of diplomatic relations between China and the United States as a critical step for China's opening and reform. Soon after he came back to power in 1977, Deng took decisive steps to work with the Carter administration to establish full diplomatic relations between the two countries in January 1979. Deng's visit to the United States in early 1979 was not only significant for improving bilateral relations but also instrumental for promoting reform and opening in China. Since the normalization of Sino-American relations, Beijing has always paid special attention to its relations with the United States. Beijing and Washington enjoyed a strategic and diplomatic honeymoon period following the normalization of relations.

From the Chinese perspective, the United States will continue to be the main diplomatic partner and competitor of China for a relatively long period of time. There is both conflict and cooperation between China and the United States. Because of the leading role of the United States in the world economy and military, development in China-U.S. relations will significantly affect China's relations with Japan and many

Western countries. The United States is China's main exporting market and a main source of capital, technology, and advanced management experience. Therefore, maintaining and developing Sino-American relations has strategic significance for China.

When he first came into power in 2001, President George W. Bush considered China a competitor rather than a strategic partner. The September 11, 2001, terrorist attack on the United States made it clear that the top threat to U.S. national security is international terrorism. In the war against terrorism, China is a partner. The Chinese leaders continue to emphasize developing a stable and constructive relationship with the United States. President Bush visited Beijing during August 8–11, 2008, and attended the opening ceremony of the 29th Olympic Games. In his meeting with President Hu Jintao, Bush said that the U.S.-China relationship is "important, constructive, and candid." Hu said that Sino-American relations have maintained a positive trend of development. The two sides maintain exchange and cooperation in the areas of trade, antiterrorism, energy, environmental protection, and law enforcement. A good and continuously improving Sino-American relationship is consistent with the fundamental interests of the people of the two countries. Such a relationship will have a far-reaching impact on the peace, stability, and prosperity of the Asia-Pacific region and even the whole world. Many policy makers in Beijing and Washington consider their bilateral relations more complex and interdependent than ever before.

U.S.-China economic ties have expanded tremendously over the last three decades. Since normalization of U.S.-Chinese relations in the 1970s, economic ties have in fact been the driving force of the bilateral relationship. The commercial relationship has served as a bridge between the two countries despite fluctuations in political relations. After three decades of rapid development, China and the United States have become truly interdependent. China's economy has never been so closely linked to the outside world before now. The United States is China's largest trading partner (unless the European Union is considered as one unit). China has emerged as the United States' second-largest trading partner. China has also become the largest foreign holder of U.S. treasury notes, with $900 billion in 2010. With other investments, China has a total of over $1 trillion invested in the United States. China has indeed become a stakeholder of the current international economic system.

Since coming into the White House in 2009, President Barack Obama has made it clear that he is determined to change American foreign policy in the Middle East, by initiating an orderly withdrawal of combatant troops from Iraq. On China policy, however, it seems that there is more continuity than change from the Bush administration to the Obama administration. In their first meeting at the G20 economic summit in London on April 1, 2009, President Obama and President Hu agreed to work together to build a "positive, cooperative, and comprehensive relationship in the 21st century." Hu said during the meeting that no matter how the situation across the Taiwan Strait evolves, China will steadfastly adhere to the one-China policy and resolutely oppose "Taiwan independence," "One China, one Taiwan," and "Two Chinas." Obama said that the U.S. government is committed to the one-China policy and the three Chinese-U.S. joint communiqués, adding that this stand will not change. The United States welcomes and supports efforts to improve relations across the strait and hopes for greater progress in those relations.

The global financial crisis that began in 2008 is a very significant development in the international community. The impact of the crisis will be felt for a long time to come. Having originated in the United States, it has created worldwide repercussions. Both China and the United States are facing tough challenges. It is clear that there is no escape from the crisis. All countries are in the same boat due to globalization. The crisis has led to a much deeper interdependence between China and the United States. The two countries need each other more than ever in confronting the global economic challenges.

The new challenges that require Chinese-U.S. cooperation are related to the following issues. First, both China and the United States have strong interest in maintaining international peace and stability in an increasingly complex regional and global environment. China and the United States continue to be two of the most important powers in East Asia. No major security issues in East Asia can be solved without input from both. Although East Asia seems relatively stable compared with the Middle East and Central Asia, the region also has its own serious problems. The most outstanding case is the ongoing North Korean nuclear crisis. At one time, comanagement of the Korean issue between China and the United States seemed quite promising under the framework of the Six Party Talks. However, Kim Jong Il has refused to give up his nuclear ambitions and has conducted multiple provocative missile tests. Both Beijing and Washington are determined to achieve denuclearization in the Korean Peninsula. An enormous amount of difficult work is required to achieve this objective. The United States tends to overestimate Beijing's influence over Pyongyang and thus wishes China would exercise more influence in the negotiation process with North Korea. China is concerned about the risk of breaking its traditionally strong ties with North Korea without achieving the objective of denuclearization. Washington wishes to avoid spending more resources in the Korean Peninsula while fighting wars in Iraq and Afghanistan. As a result, the United States has demonstrated more patience in using the diplomatic approach in Korea than in other places. Cooperation between China and the United States is essential for any viable solution of the North Korean nuclear crisis. Taking a long-term approach to East Asian stability, the contending views over Japan's historical role in Asia versus the current Japanese demand of becoming a "normal" country might become a serious challenge to both China and the United States. As a victim of Japan's past aggression, China is naturally concerned over any militaristic orientation of Japan. If Beijing, Washington, and Tokyo can achieve mutual understanding on this issue, East Asia will have a better chance of remaining stable. From Tokyo and Washington's view, however, China's modernization is cause for concern about what Beijing might do when China becomes even stronger in the future. As a result of the growing tensions in the Korean Peninsula, Japan and the United States have strengthened their security cooperation in recent times. The United States also wishes that Seoul and Tokyo would enhance their cooperation. But the history of Japan's invasion and colonial rule of Korea and the current differences between the two countries make closer cooperation between South Korea and Japan very difficult to achieve.

Second, the global financial crisis has made it clear that China and the United States are in the same boat of globalization. The financial crisis that originated in the subprime lending crisis in the United States has not only severely damaged Wall Street but also has had a very negative impact on the global economy. Over 20 million Chinese workers lost their jobs in 2008. The U.S. federal government and the PRC central government have initiated the world's two largest economic stimulus plans. Global financial crisis demands international cooperation, and close cooperation between Beijing and Washington is especially critical for resolving the current financial crisis. The Obama administration believes that China should be more flexible in allowing the value of the yuan to rise to reflect its true value. In response to those demands, China has allowed the yuan to appreciate from the old rate of U.S. $1 to 8.3 yuan (1994–2005) to about U.S. $1 to 6.5 yuan in April 2011. Some Chinese economists are concerned that the rising value of the yuan plus growing inflation might reduce the competitiveness of Chinese products in the world market. Some Western scholars and policy makers, however, argue that China should continue to allow the value of the yuan to rise to reflect its true value.

Third, Beijing and Washington have become strategic partners of antiterrorism. Since September 11, 2001, antiterrorism has become the central security challenge for the United States. China is an indispensible partner in the international fight against terrorism. China is also a victim of international terrorist attacks, such as the bombings of buses in Xinjiang conducted by the extremist East Turkistan Islamic Movement terrorists in recent years and the Urumqi riots by "separatists" in July 2009. At the strategic level, both Beijing and Washington are clearly against terrorism. At the operational level, however, there is ambiguity about who is and who is not a terrorist. The U.S. Department of State has listed the East Turkistan Islamic Movement as a terrorist group. When the U.S. administration considers releasing Xinjiang Uyghur suspects caught by the U.S. military in Afghanistan and held at Guantanamo Bay, the United States is unwilling to release them to China for concerns about possible rough treatment against them. It is likely that in the future China and the United States will more closely cooperate in the joint effort against terrorism and other international crimes.

Fourth, the Taiwan issue has long been considered one of the biggest challenges for Beijing and Washington. There has been meaningful and concrete progress in improving relations across the Taiwan Strait. China and the United States have adopted some informal comanagement of the Taiwan issue. The United States has publicly stated its position against Taiwan independence. With power in Taiwan having changed from the proindependence Democratic Progressive Party to the pro–status quo Nationalist Party in 2008, a precious opportunity for building cross-strait peace has emerged. Washington welcomes the positive development in cross-strait relations. Although differences remain between Beijing and Washington on the U.S. arms sale to Taiwan, improved mutual understanding will help to improve cross-strait exchange. Substantial improvement in cross-strait relations will enable Beijing and Washington to build a stronger strategic relationship in the future. It is interesting that President Obama and President Hu Jintao did not highlight the Taiwan issue during their January 2011 summit in Washington. Perhaps this is an indication that Beijing and Washington feel that the Taiwan issue is well managed. It is important for both sides to work closely to prevent the Taiwan issue from becoming a source of conflict.

Fifth, China's modernization has significantly benefited from a dynamic and rapidly growing relationship with the United States. At the same time, success in China's rapid economic growth has enabled the rapid growth of Sino-American economic relations, both in quality and quantity. Over the last three decades, China has learned many valuable lessons from the experience of the United States in economic development. With the global financial crisis, many Chinese are reexamining the Chinese system and the U.S. system. Perhaps Americans can also take a close look at the Chinese socioeconomic system to see if the United States can learn something from China's best practices. Some analysts have pointed out that the Chinese save too much and the Americans consume too much. If this is true, the Americans might learn how to save more and achieve a more balanced budget instead of relying heavily on deficit financing. Of course, if the Americans learn this lesson too quickly and too well, the global market might confront the challenge of weak consumer demand for many categories of goods. With China's success in economic modernization, environmental degradation has been growing. As a result, China and the United States are facing unprecedented challenges in coping with global climate change and reducing natural resource waste. This presents both risks and opportunities. If Beijing and Washington keep blaming each other and cannot achieve mutual understanding and cooperation, the global environment will continue to deteriorate at an accelerating pace. There will be no hope of sustainable growth whatsoever if China and the United States do not take active and measurable steps to reduce carbon dioxide emissions. On the other hand, if the two countries can take significant and meaningful measures to promote green development and build a healthy environment, they can set great examples for the rest of the world. China and the United States have a responsibility to lead international efforts in promoting green energy and sustainable development. This can be a win-win game.

During President Hu Jintao's state visit to the United States in January 2011, President Obama stressed that the "positive, constructive, cooperative U.S.-China relationship is good for the United States." President Obama and President Hu highlighted specific ways to cooperate on a variety of global and bilateral challenges, including the following: (1) establishing a center for excellence in nuclear security; (2) enhancing cooperation on climate change, clean energy, and the environment; (3) strengthening science and technology cooperation; (4) promoting educational exchange; (5) establishing a public private partnership on health care; and (6) establishing a U.S.-China Governors Forum to promote peer-to-peer exchanges between U.S. governors and Chinese provincial party secretaries and governors on topics of mutual concern, such as trade and investment, energy and the environment, tourism, and education.[6]

Since the 1980s, the United States has been the most popular destination for Chinese students to pursue advanced studies. With a growing middle class with strong emphasis on higher education, China has more students studying in America than any other country. President Obama launched an initiative in November 2009 to reach the goal of 100,000 American students studying in China in the near future. China has responded positively by providing some scholarships for American students to study in China. Such educational exchanges play an important role in promoting mutual understanding and friendship between citizens of the two countries.

As a result of China's modernization and the development of U.S.-China relations, China's role in world affairs is changing. In 1978 China was a developing country that had just started reform and opening to the outside world. The gap between the GDP of China and the United States in 1978 was more than 13 times. By 2010, however, China emerged as the world's second-largest economy. The U.S. GDP in 2010 ($14.7 trillion) was only two and one-half times that of China ($5.87 trillion). More significantly, in terms of contribution to global economic growth, China has become the most significant emerging economy in the world. China is becoming more and more active in all major international organizations. In 2009 China surpassed Germany as the world's largest exporting country. In 2010, China's GDP exceeded that of Japan to become the second-largest in the world. If China successfully rises to the challenges of globalization, including the latest international financial crisis, it will play an even greater role in the global community in the future.

THE FUTURE OF CHINA'S POLITICS

The future of China's politics depends on both its internal development and its interaction with the outside world. It seems that domestic sources are driving China's strategy of peaceful development. China's dynamic growth and peaceful relations with the outside world have indicated that the strategic choice made by Deng Xiaoping and his supporters was correct. China's peaceful development requires deep reform that will provide both institutional and technological innovation. Over the last three decades, China has made enormous progress and built a firm foundation for developing into a great power in the future. At the same time, China has accumulated a large number of domestic problems while going through a series of profound changes. These problems include rising unemployment, rampant official corruption, a weak legal system, growing regional disparity, a growing gap between the rich and the poor, unequal access to education, population problems, energy bottlenecks, and severe environmental problems. If these critical problems cannot be solved or alleviated effectively, they may cause crises and lead to calamitous impacts on political and social stability. In recent times, Chinese citizens often list corruption, bureaucratism, increase in unemployment and laid-off workers, inflation, and the widening gap between the rich and the poor as the main factors affecting social stability in China.

The tough problems that China is confronting today can only be resolved through the deepening of reform. Widespread corruption has in fact weakened the Chinese government's managerial ability, but the Chinese political system still retains certain mobilization power. The Chinese leadership may prevent a major social crisis if it properly manages politics, implements system innovation, overcomes corruption and polarization, and distributes the fruits of economic growth more rationally among all social members. If the reformers improve the supervision system effectively, via democratic construction at the basic level, and pursue a checks and balances mechanism for internal party power, China will move in the direction of democratization with Chinese characteristics. Over the long run, democracy might be the only way for the regime to sustain legitimacy. It is important to examine the transition from a revolutionary party to a governing party and democracy under the new leadership. Renewed debate in China about democracy and numerous local democratic elections might lead to fresh efforts at building a new political order.

In the future, fundamental political change could start from grassroots democratization and intraparty democracy, moving to a more open and free type of election at higher levels of government. There will be no real checks and balances without democracy. Without checks and balances, there will be no real solution to corruption, and there will be no real peace and stability in China over the long run. Suppression works temporarily, but not for the long term; additionally, the cost is too high and it undermines the credibility and legitimacy of the government. That is why deep reform is necessary. "Deep reform" is not simply "rectification of party discipline," a "mass line," or "people-oriented" propaganda, but rather it is real political reform—not simply "administrative" in nature but "political" in nature—transforming the relationship between the party and the government, between the party leaders and the rank-and-file members, and between the government and the citizens.[7] Such fundamental political reform will also continue to affect the international environment of China.

Deep reform and peaceful development are mutually supportive and mutually enabling. If deep reform fails, China's peaceful development will be interrupted. If peaceful development is blocked or interrupted, deep reform will suffer a serious setback. The symbiotic relationship between peaceful development and deep reform requires China to simultaneously deepen its domestic reforms and pursue a peaceful diplomacy. The ultimate success of this grand strategy of peaceful development demands not only the persistent hard work of many generations of Chinese people but also a true spirit of cooperation from the other great powers.

Peaceful development represents the dream of the Chinese people to achieve prosperity and power in a peaceful environment. This is a dream of growing prosperity, a healthy environment, social harmony, diverse culture, dynamic interaction with the outside world, and friendly and peaceful relations with all countries. This dream is consistent with the common aspiration of the majority of people in the world. In reality, China's development is not smooth. Power transition in international politics has always presented serious challenges for both the rising power and the dominant power.[8] In this context, China's peaceful development presents fresh challenges to both scholars and policy makers. In fact, the Chinese reformers may very well be taking a road not traveled yet and creating a new path of development.

China today confronts multiple challenges, including resource constraints, environmental degradation, shortage of skilled laborers, weak social security, a weak health safety net, deficits in social trust, and diminishing returns on investment. A fascinating fact is that China continues to move ahead rapidly in spite of daunting challenges. Many times alarmists have proclaimed the "coming collapse of China." Such crisis calls have repeatedly turned out to be overstated. It seems reasonable to argue that Chinese reality is somewhere between the model of economic "miracle" and the warning of "crisis" or "collapse." The drive to achieve peaceful development and the fear of growing crisis are both powerful motivating forces for China's reformers to carry out deep reform. As careful analysts have pointed out, motivations can change, and history shows how motivational change of a rising great power can wreak havoc in world politics. Ultimately, much of the international confidence in China's intentions depends on its firm embrace of international responsibility and domestic reforms. The fundamental goal of deep reform is to restructure the Chinese political and economic systems in order to adapt to a changing international environment.

Most studies of the rise of China are based on the assumption that the Chinese economy will continue to grow at high rate in the foreseeable future. However, there is no guarantee that China will be able to maintain sustainable growth over the long run.[9] The growing environmental pressure, resource constraints, and demographic shifts in China might put a brake to the high growth rate. At the same time, issues of corruption, social disparity, and potential social unrest all make the situation more complicated. At the March 2011 National People's Congress meeting, Premier Wen Jiabao envisioned China's GDP growth rate during the next five years to be 7 percent a year. The new emphasis is on quality over speed of economic development, with more attention on improving people's lives. This is consistent with the scientific development outlook. It remains to be seen whether such objectives can be achieved. It will be very difficult to change the deeply entrenched GDP-first mentality.

Since the 1911 revolution, China has experienced several major revolutions and different patterns of modernization. Students of Chinese politics have been surprised repeatedly at the twists and turns of China's socioeconomic development and political change.[10] China is still searching for its rightful place in the world. What remains true is that China's past will continue to affect its future. The Chinese political system will continue to evolve as the country continues to modernize in a changing world. China must adjust its development strategy according to changing circumstance at home and abroad. The outside world also needs to respond to the rise of China as a world power.

Notes

1. Marc Blecher, *China against the Tides: Restructuring through Revolution, Radicalism and Reform.* 3rd ed. (New York, Continuum: 2010), 2.

2. Harry Harding, *Organizing China: The Problem of Bureaucracy, 1949–1976.* (Stanford, CA: Stanford University Press, 1981).

3. Kenneth Lieberthal, "The Great Leap Forward and the Split in the Yanan leadership, 1958–65," in *The Politics of China: The Eras of Mao and Deng*, ed. Roderick MacFarquhar, 2nd ed. (New York: Cambridge University Press, 1997), 98.

4. Lowell Dittmer, *China's Continuous Revolution: The Post-Liberation Epoch, 1949–1981* (Berkeley, CA: University of California Press, 1989), 35–36.

5. Roderick MacFarquhar and Michael Schoenhals, *Mao's Last Revolution* (Cambridge, MA: Harvard University Press, 2006), 460.

CHAPTER 2

1. Philip Short, *Mao: A Life* (New York: Henry Holt and Company, 1999).

2. Mao Zedong, *Selected Works of Mao Tse-Tung*, vol. 1 (Peking: Foreign Language Press, 1967), 23–24.

3. Jiang Zemin, *Jiang Zemin Wenxuan*, vol. 3 (Beijing: Renmin Chubanshe, 2006), 2.

4. Cheng Li, "China's Communist Party-State: The Structure and Dynamics of Power," in *Politics in China: An Introduction*, ed. William A. Joseph (New York: Oxford University Press, 2010), 179.

5. Kevin J. O'Brien and Lianjiang Li, *Rightful Resistance in Rural China* (New York: Cambridge University Press, 2006).

6. For an interesting analysis of Hu Jintao and his colleagues, see Cheng Li, *China's Leaders: The New Generation* (Lanham, MD: Rowman and Little-field Publishers, 2001).

7. Willy Wo-Lap Lam, *Chinese Politics in the Hu Jintao Era: New Leaders, New Challenges* (Armonk, NY: M.E. Sharpe, 2006) 10.

8. Deng Xiaoping, "Speech to Comrades Who Had Attended an Enlarged Meeting of the Military Commission of the Central Committee of the Communist Party of China," November 12, 1989, in *Selected Works of Deng Xiaoping*, vol. 3, *1982–1992* (Beijing: Foreign Languages Press, 1994). Available at http://web.peopledaily.com.cn/english/dengxp/vol3/text/d1070.html, accessed December 5, 2010.

CHAPTER 3

1. David Shambaugh, *China's Communist Party: Atrophy and Adaptation* (Washington, D.C.: Woodrow Wilson Center Press; Berkeley, CA: University of California Press, 2008), 7.

2. Interview with Wen Jiabao, CNN, http://transcripts.cnn.com/TRANSCRIPTS/1010/03/fzgps.01.html, accessed October 15, 2010.

3. Cheng Li, "China's Communist Party-State: The Structure and Dynamics of Power," in *Politics in China: An Introduction*, ed. William A. Joseph (New York: Oxford University Press, 2010), 167–168.

4. Ibid., 168.

5. Ibid.

6. Ibid., 169. For a detailed analysis of the CCP from the perspective of a reporter for the *Financial Times*, see Richard McGregor, *The Party: The Secret World of China's Communist Rulers* (New York: Harper, 2010).

7. McGregor, *The Party*, vi–vii.

8. Tony Saich, *Governance and Politics of China*, 2nd ed. (New York: Palgrave Macmillan, 2004), 104.

9. Kenneth Lieberthal, *Governing China: From Revolution through Reform*, 2nd ed. (New York: W.W. Norton, 2004), 241.

10. Deng Xiaoping, "Upholding the Four Cardinal Principles," March 30, 1979, in *Selected Works of Deng Xiaoping*, vol. 2. (Beijing: Foreign Language

Press, 1995). Available at http://english.peopledaily.com.cn/dengxp/vol2/text/b1290.html, accessed January 2, 2011.

11. Jiang Zemin, *Jiang Zemin Wenxuan*, vol. 3 (Beijing: Renmin Chubanshe, 2006), 2.

12. William A. Joseph, "Ideology and Chinese Politics," in *Politics in China*, 158.

13. Andrew Scobell, *Chinese Army Building in the Era of Jiang Zemin*, Strategic Studies Institute, U.S. Army War College, August 2000, 11. Available at http://www.strategicstudiesinstitute.army.mil/pdffiles/pub69.pdf, accessed January 3, 2011.

14. Joseph, "Ideology and Chinese Politics," in *Politics in China,* 159.

15. Author's interview with a party secretary in southern Guizhou, March 10, 2008.

16. Yu Keping, *Democracy Is a Good Thing: Essays on Politics, Society, and Culture in Contemporary China* (Washington, D.C.: Brookings Institution Press, 2008).

17. Zhou Tianyong and Wang Changjiang, *Gongjian: A Report on Political Reform in China after the 17th Party Congress* (Xinjiang, China: Xinjiang Production and Building Corps Press, 2007).

18. Chris Buckley, "China Premier Wen Calls for Political Reform," Reuters, August 22, 2010, http://www.reuters.com/article/idUSTRE67L0AL20100822, accessed November 1, 2010.

19. Ibid.

20. Ibid.

21. Raymond Zhou, "Why Is China Angry?" *China Daily*, April 24, 2009, http://www.chinadaily.com.cn/opinion/2009-04/24/content_7710542.htm, accessed November 2, 2010.

22. Randall Peerenboom, *China Modernizes: Threat to the West or Model for the Rest?* (New York: Oxford University Press, 2007), 284.

CHAPTER 4

1. Cheng Li, "China's Communist Party-State: The Structure and Dynamics of Power," in *Politics in China: An Introduction*, ed. William A. Joseph (New York: Oxford University Press, 2010), 175.

2. Cai Dingjian, "Citizen Participation and Government Decisionmaking," [in Chinese], China Elections and Governance.org, http://www.chinaelections.org/NewsInfo.asp?NewsID=193566, accessed December 5, 2010.

3. "Reduce Administrative Costs," March 30, 2010, *China Daily*, March 30, 2010, http://www.chinadaily.com.cn/opinion/2010-03/30/content_9660209.htm, accessed November 6, 2010.

4. Yongnian Zheng, "Central-Local Relations: The Power to Dominate," in *China Today, China Tomorrow: Domestic Politics, Economy, and Society*, ed. Joseph Fewsmith (Lanham, MD: Rowman and Littlefield, 2010), 193–194.

5. John Bryan Starr, *Understanding China: A Guide to China's Economy, History, and Political Culture*, 3rd ed. (New York: Hill and Wang, 2010), 71.

6. Ibid., 60.

7. Ibid., 128.

8. Kenneth Lieberthal, *Governing China: From Revolution through Reform*, 2nd ed. (New York: W.W. Norton, 2004), 186–187.

9. Starr, *Understanding China*, 64.

10. "1.4M Sit China's Civil Service Exam," *People's Daily*, December 6, 2010, http://english.peopledaily.com.cn/90001/90776/90882/7221319.html, accessed December 10, 2010.

CHAPTER 5

1. See World Bank, *World Development Indicators 2005*; and *World Development Indicators 2010*, 92. Available at http://data.worldbank.org/sites/default/files/wdi-final.pdf, accessed December 6, 2010.

2. See Lowell Dittmer and Guoli Liu, eds., *China's Deep Reform: Domestic Politics in Transition* (Lanham, MD: Rowman and Littlefield, 2006).

3. Loren Brandt and Thomas G. Rawski, "China's Great Economic Transformation," in *China's Great Economic Transformation*, ed. Loren Brandt and Thomas G. Rawski (New York: Cambridge University Press, 2008), 2.

4. Barry Naughton, *Growing Out of the Plan* (New York: Cambridge University Press, 1995); and Barry Naughton, *The Chinese Economy: Transitions and Growth* (Cambridge, MA: MIT Press, 2007).

5. Lord Acton, Letter to Mandell Creighton, April 3, 1887. Available at http://oll.libertyfund.org/index.php?option=com_content&task=view&id=1407&Itemid=283, accessed December 6, 2010.

6. Justin Yifu Lin, Fan Cai, and Zhou Li, *The China Miracle: Development Strategy and Economic Reform* (Hong Kong: The Chinese University Press, 1996), 271.

7. Merle Goldman and Roderick MacFarquhar, "Dynamic Economy, Declining Party-State," in *The Paradox of China's Post-Mao Reforms*, ed. Merle Goldman and Roderick MacFarquhar (Cambridge, MA: Harvard University Press, 1999), 29.

8. Pingyao Lai, "China's Foreign Trade: Achievements, Determinants and Future Policy Challenges," *China & World Economy* 12: 6 (2004), 38–50. For a systematic and thorough analysis of China's foreign trade policy, see Nicholas R. Lardy, *Foreign Trade and Economic Reform in China, 1978–1990* (New York: Cambridge University Press, 1992); and Nicholas R. Lardy, *Integrating China into the Global Economy* (Washington, D.C.: Brookings Institution Press, 2002).

9. See Lowell Dittmer and Guoli Liu, eds., *China's Deep Reform: Domestic Politics in Transition* (Lanham, MD: Rowman and Littlefield, 2006).

10. Hong Zhang, "Woguo Duwai Maoyi Jigou jiqu Bijiao Youshi de Shizheng Fengxi" (An Empirical Study of China's Comparative Advantage and Structure in Foreign Trade), *Guoji Maoyi Wenti* 4 (2006), 50.

11. Dani Rodrik, "What's So Special about China's Exports?" (Revised January 2006). See http://www.hks.harvard.edu/fs/drodrik/Research%20papers/Chinaexports.pdf, accessed January 3, 2011.

12. Deng Xiaoping, "On the Reform of the System of Party and State Leadership," in *Selected Works of Deng Xiaoping*, vol. 2, *1975–1982* (Beijing: Foreign Languages Press, 1995), 316.

13. See Peter Beaumont, "Wen Jiabao Puts Political Reform on China's Agenda," *The Observer*, August 29, 2010. http://www.guardian.co.uk/world/2010/aug/29/wen-jiabao-china-reform, accessed November 3, 2010.

14. Wu Jinglian is a senior research associate at the Development Research Center of the State Council (a major think tank for the central government). Since the early 1980s, he has been a strong advocate for building a market economy in China. He is the author of *Understanding and Interpreting Chinese Economic Reform*. Mason, OH: Thomson/South-Western, 2005.

15. James R. Townsend and Brantly Womack, *Politics in China*, 3rd ed. (Glenview, IL: Scott, Foresman, 1986), 394.

16. John Bryan Starr, *Understanding China: A Guide to China's Economy, History, and Political Culture*, 3rd ed. (New York: Hill and Wang, 2010), 99.

17. Ibid., 103.

18. Yasheng Huang, *Capitalism with Chinese Characteristics: Entrepreneurship and the State* (New York: Cambridge University Press, 2008).

19. Richard Baum, *Burying Mao: Chinese Politics in the Age of Deng Xiaoping* (Princeton, NJ: Princeton University Press, 1996), 361.

20. Deborah Davis and Wang Feng, "Poverty and Wealth in Postsocialist China: An Overview," in *Creating Wealth and Poverty in Postsocialist China*, ed. Deborah Davis and Wang Feng (Stanford, CA: Stanford University Press, 2009), 6.

21. Carl Riskin, Zhao Renwei, and Li Shi, eds., *China's Retreat from Equality: Income Distribution and Economic Transition* (Armonk, NY: M.E. Sharpe, 2001), 3.

22. Zhao Renwei, "Increasing Income Inequality and Its Causes in China," in *China's Retreat from Equality,* 27, 31.

23. Carl Riskin and Li Shi, "Chinese Rural Poverty Inside and Outside the Poor Regions," in *China's Retreat from Equality,* 329–344.

24. Starr, *Understanding China,* 103.

25. Richard Dobbs, "Megacities: *Foreign Policy*'s Guide to the Coming Urban Age," *Foreign Policy,* September/October 2010, http://www. foreignpolicy.com/articles/2010/08/16/prime_numbers_megacities?page=full, accessed December 2, 2010.

26. Dan Steinbock, "China's Urbanization: It Has Only Just Begun," *New Geography,* December 2, 2010, http://www.newgeography.com/content/ 001906-china%E2%80%99s-urbanization-it-has-only-just-begun, accessed December 6, 2010.

27. Chak Kwan Chan, King Lun Ngok, and David Phillips, *Social Policy in China: Development and Well-being* (Bristol, U.K.: The Policy Press, 2008), 115–117.

28. "China 'Fake Milk' Scandal Deepens," BBC News, April 22, 2004, http://news.bbc.co.uk/2/hi/asia-pacific/3648583.stm, accessed November 5, 2010.

29. Jessie Jiang, "China's Rage over Toxic Baby Milk," *Time,* September 19, 2008, http://www.time.com/time/world/article/0,8599,1842727,00.html, accessed November 6, 2010.

30. Joanna Lewis, "Environmental Challenges: From the Local to the Global," in *China Today, China Tomorrow: Domestic Politics, Economy, and Society,* ed. Joseph Fewsmith (Lanham, MD: Rowman and Littlefield, 2010), 260.

31. Elizabeth C. Economy, *The River Runs Black: The Environmental Challenges to China's Future* (Ithaca, NY: Cornell University Press, 2004).

CHAPTER 6

1. *The Analects of Confucius: A Philosophical Translation,* trans. Roger T. Ames and Henry Rosemont, Jr. (New York: Ballantine Books, 1998); Zhengyuan Fu, *China's Legalists: The Earliest Totalitarians and Their Art of Ruling* (Armonk, NY: M.E. Sharpe, 1996); Xinzhong Yao, "Fa and Law: A Critical Examination of the Confucian and Legalist Approaches to Law," http://

tkugloba.tku.edu.tw/english/doc-e/AFa%20and%20Law.htm, accessed December 1, 2010.

2. Chunying Xin, *Chinese Legal System and Current Legal Reform* (Beijing: Legal Press, 1999), 310–313.

3. Yong Zhang, ed., *Comparative Studies on the Judicial Review System in East and Southeast Asia* (The Hague, Netherlands: Kluwer Law International, 1997), 70.

4. *People's Daily*, September 13, 1997.

5. Jiang Zemin, "Speech at the National Propaganda Working Conference," *Guangmin ribao*, January 11, 2001, 3.

6. Zou Keyuan, "The Party and the Law," in *The Chinese Communist Party in Reform*, ed. Kjeld Erik Brodsgaard and Zheng Yongnian (New York: Routledge, 2006), 87.

7. Randall Peerenboom, *China Modernizes: Threat to the West or Model for the Rest?* New York: Oxford University Press, 2007, 195.

8. For a comparative analysis of 10 countries, see Daniel P. Franklin and Michael J. Baum, eds., *Political Culture and Constitutionalism: A Comparative Approach* (Armonk, NY: M.E. Sharpe, 1995).

9. Malcolm Moore, "China Spends Record Amount Targeting Domestic Security Threats," London: *The Telegraph*, March 29, 2010.

10. Jerome A. Cohen, "China's Reform Era Legal Odyssey," *Far Eastern Economic Review*, 34 (December 2008), 35–38.Xuehua Zhang, Leonard Ortolano, and Zhongmei Lu, "Agency Empowerment through the Administrative Litigation Law: Court Enforcement of Pollution Levies in Hubei Province," *The China Quarterly* 202 (2010), 307–326.

11. Zhao Bingzhi and Wan Yunfeng, "On Limiting and Abolishing the Death Penalty for Economic Crimes in China," *Chinese Sociology and Anthropology* 41: 4 (Summer 2009), 14–40.

12. Susan Trevaskes, "Courts on the Campaign Path in China: Criminal Court Work in the 'Yanda 2001' Anti-Crime Campaign," *Asian Survey* 42: 5 (2002), 678.

13. "Former Police Chief Wen Qiang Executed," *People's Daily*, July 7, 2010, http://english.peopledaily.com.cn/90001/90776/90882/7056102.html, accessed November 17, 2010.

14. *Peking Review*, December 29, 1978, 14.

15. Deng Xiaoping, *Selected Works of Deng Xiaoping*, vol. 2, *1975–1982* (Beijing: Foreign Languages Press, 1995), 158.

16. *People's Daily*, October 7, 1999.

17. Randall Peerenboom, *China's Long March toward Rule of Law* (New York: Cambridge University Press, 2002).

18. Andrew Wedeman, "Strategic Repression and Regime Stability in China's Peaceful Development," in *China's "Peaceful Rise" in the 21st Century*, ed. Sujian Guo (Aldershot, England: Ashgate, 2007), 89.

19. Joseph Y. S. Cheng, ed., *Challenges and Policy Programs of China's New Leadership* (Hong Kong: City University of Hong Kong Press, 2007), 2.

20. See Elizabeth J. Perry and Mark Selden, eds., *Chinese Society: Change, Conflict and Resistance* 2nd ed. (New York: Routledge, 2000).

21. Merle Goldman, *From Comrade to Citizen: The Struggle for Political Rights in China* (Cambridge, MA: Harvard University Press, 2005), 233.

22. Jamie Horsley, "The Rule of Law: Pushing the Limits of Party Rule," in *China Today, China Tomorrow: Domestic Politics, Economy, and Society*, ed. Joseph Fewsmith (Lanham, MD: Rowman and Littlefield, 2010), 53, 58.

23. Yan Sun, *Corruption and Market in Contemporary China* (Ithaca, NY: Cornell University Press, 2004). This book examines numerous cases of corruption during China's transition to the market in comparative perspectives.

24. John Bryan Starr, *Understanding China: A Guide to China's Economy, History, and Political Culture*, 3rd ed. (New York: Hill and Wang, 2010), 79–80.

25. Ibid., 80.

26. Dali Yang, "The Struggle against Corruption," in *Interpreting China's Development*, ed. Guangwu Wang and John Wong (Singapore: World Scientific, 2007), 38–43.

27. Ting Gong, "New Trends in China's Corruption: Change amid Continuity," in *China's Deep Reform: Domestic Politics in Transition*, ed. Lowell Dittmer and Guoli Liu (Lanham, MD: Rowman and Littlefield, 2006), 452–457.

28. Ibid., 458–459.

29. Ibid., 461–463.

30. Minxin Pei, "Fighting Corruption: A Difficult Challenge for Chinese Leaders," in *China's Changing Political Landscape: Prospects for Democracy*, ed. Cheng Li (Washington, D.C.: Brookings Institution Press, 2008), 229–230.

31. Zou Keyuan, "Towards the Rule of Law," in *Interpreting China's Development*, ed. Guangwu Wang and John Wong (Singapore: World Scientific, 2007), 56.

32. Peerenboom, *China Modernizes*, 195–198.

33. Jacques deLisle, "Legalization without Democratization in China under Hu Jintao," in *China's Changing Political Landscape: Prospects for Democracy*, ed. Cheng Li (Washington, D.C.: Brookings Institution Press, 2008), 185–190.

34. Horsley, "The Rule of Law: Pushing the Limits of Party Rule," in *China Today, China Tomorrow*, 67–68.

CHAPTER 7

1. Portions of this chapter were developed from the following articles: "Domestic Sources of China's Emerging Grand Strategy," *Journal of Asian and African Studies* 43: 5 (October 2008), 543–561 (Sage Publications); "Managing the Challenges of Complex Interdependence: China and the United States in the Era of Globalization," *Asian Politics & Policy* 2: 1 (January/March 2010), 1–23 (Wiley Publications), coauthored with Quansheng Zhao; and "The Challenge of a Rising China," *Journal of Strategic Studies* 30: 4–5 (August–October 2007), 585–608 (Routledge, Taylor and Francis Group), coauthored with Quansheng Zhao. I would like to thank Quansheng Zhao for his contribution.

2. C. Fred Bergsten, Charles Freeman, Nicholas R. Lardy, and Derek Mitchell, *China's Rise: Challenges and Opportunities* (Washington, D.C.: Peterson Institute for International Economics and Center for Strategic and International Studies, 2008); Robert S. Ross and Zhu Feng, eds., *China's Ascent: Power, Security, and the Future of International Politics* (Ithaca, NY: Cornell University Press, 2008).

3. See Herbert S. Yee, ed., *China's Rise—Threat or Opportunity?* (New York: Routledge, 2010); David C. Kang, *China Rising: Peace, Power, and Order in East Asia* (New York: Columbia University Press, 2007); and Quansheng Zhao and Guoli Liu, eds., *Managing the China Challenge* (New York: Routledge, 2009).

4. Dai Bingguo, "Stick to the Path of Peaceful Development," *China Daily*, December 13, 2010 http://www.chinadaily.com.cn/opinion/2010-12/13/content_11690133.htm, accessed December 15, 2010.

5. See Ye Zicheng, *Inside China's Grand Strategy: The Perspective from the People's Republic*, ed. and trans. Steven I. Levine and Guoli Liu (Lexington, KY: University Press of Kentucky, 2011).

6. http://www.whitehouse.gov/the-press-office/2011/01/19/us-china-building-positive-cooperative-and-comprehensive-relationship, accessed January 20, 2011.

7. See Lowell Dittmer and Guoli Liu, eds., *China's Deep Reform: Domestic Politics in Transition* (Lanham, MD: Rowman and Littlefield, 2006).

8. Avery Goldstein, *Rising to the Challenge: China's Grand Strategy and International Security* (Stanford, CA: Stanford University Press, 2005); Steve Chan, *China, the U.S., and the Power-Transition Theory* (New York:

Routledge, 2008); and Edward Friedman, "Power Transition Theory: A Challenger to the Peaceful Rise of World Power China," in *China's Rise—Threat or Opportunity?*, 11–32.

9. See Dwight H. Perkins and Thomas G. Rawski, "Forecasting China's Economic Growth to 2025," in *China's Great Economic Transformation*, ed. Loren Brandt and Thomas G. Rawski (New York: Cambridge University Press, 2008), 829–886. Perkins and Rawski believe that the Chinese economy will continue along a path of rapid growth in the coming decade. Their forecast envisions annual growth averaging 6–8 percent in real terms.

10. Jonathan D. Spence, *The Search for Modern China* (New York: W.W. Norton, 1990); Roderick MacFarquhar, ed., *The Politics of China: The Eras of Mao and Deng*, 2nd ed. (New York: Cambridge University Press, 1997); and Brantly Womack, ed., *China's Rise in Historical Perspective* (Lanham, MD: Rowman and Littlefield, 2010).

Selected Bibliography

Ash, Robert, David Shambaugh, and Seiichiro Takagi, eds. *China Watching: Perspectives from Europe, Japan and the United States.* New York: Routledge, 2007.

Baum, Richard. *Burying Mao: Chinese Politics in the Age of Deng Xiaoping.* Princeton, NJ: Princeton University Press, 1996.

Bergsten, C. Fred, Charles Freeman, Nicholas R. Lardy, and Derek J. Mitchell. *China's Rise: Challenges and Opportunities.* Washington, D.C.: Peter G. Peterson Institute for International Economics, 2008.

Bianco, Lucien. *The Origins of the Chinese Revolution, 1915–1949.* Stanford, CA: Stanford University Press, 1971.

Blecher, Marc. *China against the Tides: Restructuring through Revolution, Radicalism and Reform.* 3rd ed. New York: Continuum, 2010.

Brandt, Loren, and Thomas G. Rawski, eds. *China's Great Economic Transformation.* New York: Cambridge University Press, 2008.

Chan, Steve. *China, the U.S., and the Power-Transition Theory.* New York: Routledge, 2008.

Chang, Leslie T. *Factory Girls: From Village to City in a Changing China.* New York: Spiegel and Grau, 2007.

Chen, Jie. *Popular Political Support in Urban China.* Stanford: Stanford University Press, 2004.

Chen Jian. *Mao's China and the Cold War.* Chapel Hill, NC: University of North Carolina Press, 2001.

Chow, Gregory C. *China's Economic Transformation*. 2nd ed. Malden, MA: Blackwell Publishing, 2007.

Davis, Deborah S. *The Consumer Revolution in Urban China*. Berkeley, CA: University of California Press, 2000.

Davis, Deborah, and Wang Feng, eds. *Creating Wealth and Poverty in Postsocialist China*. Stanford, CA: Stanford University Press, 2009.

Deng Xiaoping. *Selected Works of Deng Xiaoping*. Vol. 2, 1975–1982. Beijing: Foreign Languages Press, 1995.

Deng Xiaoping. *Selected Works of Deng Xiaoping*. Vol. 3, 1982–1992. Beijing: Foreign Languages Press, 1994.

Dickson, Bruce. *Red Capitalists in China: The Party, Private Entrepreneurs, and Prospects for Change*. New York: Cambridge University Press, 2003.

Dickson, Bruce. *Wealth into Power: The Chinese Communist Party's Embrace of China's Private Sector*. New York: Cambridge University Press, 2008.

Dittmer, Lowell. *China under Reform*. Boulder, CO: Westview Press, 1994.

Dittmer, Lowell. *Liu Shaoqi and the Chinese Cultural Revolution*. (Revised edition). Armonk, NY: M.E. Sharpe, 1998.

Dittmer, Lowell, and Guoli Liu, eds. *China's Deep Reform: Domestic Politics in Transition*. Lanham, MD: Rowman and Littlefield, 2006.

Dittmer, Lowell, and George T. Yu, eds. *China, the Developing World, and the New Global Dynamic*. Boulder, CO: Lynne Rienner, 2010.

Dreyer, June Teufel. *China's Political System: Modernization and Tradition*. 7th ed. New York: Pearson Longman, 2010.

Economy, Elizabeth C. *The River Runs Black: The Environmental Challenges to China's Future*. Ithaca, NY: Cornell University Press, 2004.

Fairbank, John King, and Merle Goldman. *China: A New History*. 2nd enlarged ed. Cambridge, MA: Harvard University Press, 2006.

Fewsmith, Joseph. *China since Tiananmen: From Deng Xiaoping to Hu Jintao*. 2nd ed. New York: Cambridge University Press, 2008.

Fewsmith, Joseph. ed. *China Today, China Tomorrow: Domestic Politics, Economy, and Society*. Lanham, MD: Rowman and Littlefield, 2010.

Goldman, Merle, and Roderick MacFarquhar, eds. *The Paradox of China's Post-Mao Reforms*. Cambridge, MA: Harvard University Press, 1999.

Goldstein, Avery. *Rising to the Challenge: China's Grand Strategy and International Security*. Stanford, CA: Stanford University Press, 2005.

Grasso, June, Jay Corrin, and Michael Kort. *Modernization and Revolution in China: From the Opium War to the Olympics*. 4th ed. Armonk, NY: M.E. Sharpe, 2009.

Gries, Peter Hays. *China's New Nationalism: Pride, Politics, and Diplomacy.* Berkeley, CA: University of California Press, 2004.

Gries, Peter Hays, and Stanley Rosen. *Chinese Politics: State, Society, and the Market.* New York: Routledge, 2010.

Harding, Harry. *China's Second Revolution: Reform after Mao.* Washington, D.C.: Brookings Institution, 1987.

Huang, Yasheng. *Capitalism with Chinese Characteristics: Entrepreneurship and the State.* New York: Cambridge University Press, 2008.

Huang, Yasheng. *Selling China: Foreign Direct Investment during the Reform Era.* New York: Cambridge University Press, 2003.

Johnston, Alastair Iain, and Robert S. Ross, eds. *New Directions in the Study of China's Foreign Policy.* Stanford, CA: Stanford University Press, 2006.

Joseph, William A., ed. *Politics in China: An Introduction.* New York: Oxford University Press, 2010.

Kang, David C. *China Rising: Peace, Power, and Order in East Asia.* New York: Columbia University Press, 2007.

Kynge, James. *China Shakes the World: A Titan's Rise and Troubled Future—and the Challenge for America.* Boston: Houghton Mifflin, 2006.

Lam, Willy Wo-Lap. *Chinese Politics in the Hu Jintao Era: New Leaders, New Challenges.* Armonk, NY: M.E. Sharpe, 2006.

Lampton, David M., ed. *The Making of Chinese Foreign and Security Policy in the Era of Reform.* Stanford: Stanford University Press, 2001.

Lardy, Nicholas R. *China's Unfinished Economic Revolution.* Washington, D.C.: Brookings Institution Press, 1998.

Lardy, Nicholas R. *Foreign Trade and Economic Reform in China, 1978–1990.* New York: Cambridge University Press, 1992.

Lardy, Nicholas R. *Integrating China into the Global Economy.* Washington, D.C.: Brookings Institution Press, 2002.

Li, Cheng, ed. *China's Changing Political Landscape: Prospects for Democracy.* Washington, D.C.: Brookings Institution Press, 2008.

Li, Cheng. *China's Leaders: The New Generation.* Lanham, MD: Rowman and Littlefield, 2001.

Lieberthal, Kenneth. *Governing China: From Revolution through Reform.* 2nd ed. New York: W.W. Norton, 2004.

Lin, Justin Yifu, Fan Cai, and Zhou Li. *The China Miracle: Development Strategy and Economic Reform.* Hong Kong: The Chinese University Press, 1996.

Luo, Jing, ed. *China Today: An Encyclopedia of Life in the People's Republic.* 2 vols. Westport: Greenwood Press, 2005.

MacFarquhar, Roderick, ed. *The Politics of China: The Eras of Mao and Deng.* 2nd ed. New York: Cambridge University Press, 1997.

MacFarquhar, Roderick, and Michael Schoenhals. *Mao's Last Revolution.* Cambridge, MA: Harvard University Press, 2008.

McGregor, Richard. *The Party: The Secret World of China's Communist Rulers.* New York: Harper, 2010.

Meredith, Robyn. *The Elephant and the Dragon: The Rise of India and China and What It Means for All of Us.* New York: W.W. Norton, 2008.

Mitter, Rana. *A Bitter Revolution: China's Struggle with the Modern World.* New York: Oxford University Press, 2005.

Naughton, Barry. *The Chinese Economy: Transitions and Growth.* Cambridge, MA: MIT Press, 2007.

Naughton, Barry. *Growing Out of the Plan.* New York: Cambridge University Press, 1995.

O'Brien, Kevin J., and Lianjiang Li. *Rightful Resistance in Rural China.* New York: Cambridge University Press, 2006.

Oi, Jean C. *Rural China Takes Off: Institutional Foundations of Economic Reform.* Berkeley, CA: University of California Press, 1999.

Organization for Economic Co-operation and Development. *China in the World Economy: The Domestic Policy Challenges.* Paris: OECD, 2002.

Peerenboom, Randall. *China Modernizes: Threat to the West or Model for the Rest?* New York: Cambridge University Press, 2007.

Peerenboom, Randall. *China's Long March toward Rule of Law.* New York: Cambridge University Press, 2002.

Pei, Minxin. *China's Trapped Transition: The Limits of Developmental Autocracy.* Cambridge, MA: Harvard University Press, 2006.

Perry, Elizabeth J., and Merle Goldman, eds. *Grassroots Political Reform in Contemporary China.* Cambridge, MA: Harvard University Press, 2007.

Perry, Elizabeth J., and Mark Selden, eds. *Chinese Society: Change, Conflict and Resistance.* 3rd ed. New York: Routledge, 2010.

Pye, Lucian W. *The Dynamics of Chinese Politics.* Cambridge, MA: Oelgeschlager Gunn and Hain, 1982.

Riskin, Carl, Zhao Renwei, and Li Shi, eds. *China's Retreat from Equality: Income Distribution and Economic Transition.* Armonk, NY: M.E. Sharpe, 2001.

Ropp, Paul S. *China in World History.* New York: Oxford University Press, 2010.

Ross, Robert S., and Zhu Feng, eds. *China's Ascent: Power, Security, and the Future of International Politics.* Ithaca, NY: Cornell University Press, 2008.

Saich, Tony. *Governance and Politics of China.* 3rd ed. New York: Palgrave Macmillan, 2011.

Saich, Tony. *Providing Public Goods in Transitional China*. New York: Palgrave Macmillan, 2008.

Selden, Mark. *China in Revolution: The Yenan Way Revisited*. Armonk, NY: M.E. Sharpe, 1995.

Selden, Mark. *The Yenan Way in Revolutionary China*. Cambridge, MA: Harvard University Press, 1971.

Shambaugh, David. *China's Communist Party: Atrophy and Adaptation*. Washington, D.C.: Woodrow Wilson Center Press; Berkeley, CA: University of California Press, 2008.

Shambaugh, David. *Modernization of China's Military: Progress, Problems, and Prospects*. Berkeley, CA: University of California Press, 2002.

Shi, Tianjian. *Political Participation in Beijing*. Cambridge, MA: Harvard University Press, 1997.

Shirk, Susan. *China: Fragile Superpower*. New York: Oxford University Press, 2007.

Smil, Vaclav. *China's Past, China's Future: Energy, Food, Environment*. London: RoutledgeCurzon, 2003.

Solinger, Dorothy J. *Contesting Citizenship in Urban China: Peasant Migrants, the State, and the Logic of the Market*. Berkeley, CA: University of California Press, 1999.

Spence, Jonathan D. *The Search for Modern China*. New York: W.W. Norton, 1990.

Starr, John Bryan. *Understanding China: A Guide to China's Economy, History, and Political Culture*. 3rd ed. New York: Hill and Wang, 2010.

Steinfeld, Edward. *Forging Reform in China: The Fate of State-Owned Industry*. New York: Cambridge University Press, 1998.

Sun, Yan. *Corruption and Market in Contemporary China*. Ithaca, NY: Cornell University Press, 2004.

Sutter, Robert. *China's Foreign Relations: Power and Policy since the Cold War*. Lanham, MD: Rowman and Littlefield, 2009.

Tsai, Kelle S. *Capitalism without Democracy: The Private Sector in Contemporary China*. Ithaca, NY: Cornell University Press, 2007.

Tsou, Tang. *The Chinese Cultural Revolution and Post-Mao Reforms: A Historical Perspective*. Chicago: University of Chicago Press, 1986.

Wang, Guangwu, and John Wong, eds. *Interpreting China's Development*. Singapore: World Scientific, 2007.

Wang, Shaoguang, and Angang Hu. *The Political Economy of Uneven Development: The Case of China*. Armonk, NY: M.E. Sharpe, 1999.

Wasserstrom, Jeffrey N. *China in the 21st Century: What Everyone Needs to Know*. New York: Oxford University Press, 2010.

Weber, Max. *Economy and Society: An Outline of Interpretive Sociology.* 2 volumes. Edited by Guenther Roth and Claus Wittich. Berkeley: University of California Press, 1978.

Max. *Economy and Society.* ed. by Guenther Roth and Claus Wittich. New York: Bedminster Press, 1968.

White, Lynn, III. *Policies of Chaos: The Organizational Causes of Violence in China's Cultural Revolution.* Princeton, NJ: Princeton University Press, 1989.

World Bank. *China and the WTO: Accession, Policy Reform, and Poverty Reduction Strategies.* Washington, D.C.: World Bank, 2004.

Wright, *Accepting Authoritarianism: State-Society Relations in China's Reform Era.* Stanford, CA: Stanford University Press, 2010.

Wu Jinglian. *Understanding and Interpreting Chinese Economic Reform.* Mason, OH: Thomson/South-Western, 2005.

Xin, Chunying. *Chinese Legal System and Current Legal Reform.* Beijing: Legal Press, 1999.

Yang, Dali. *Remaking of the Chinese Leviathan: Market, Transition and the Politics of Governance in China.* Stanford, CA: Stanford University Press, 2004.

Ye, Zicheng. *Inside China's Grand Strategy: The View from the People's Republic.* Edited and translated by Steven I. Levine and Guoli Liu. Lexington, KY: The University Press of Kentucky, 2011.

Yee, Herbert S., ed. *China's Rise—Threat or Opportunity?* New York: Routledge, 2010.

Yu Keping, *Democracy Is a Good Thing: Essays on Politics, Society, and Culture in Contemporary China.* Washington, D.C.: Brookings Institution Press, 2008.

Zhao, Quansheng, and Guoli Liu, eds. *Managing the China Challenge.* New York: Routledge, 2009.

Zhao Ziyang. *Prisoner of the State: The Secret Journal of Premier Zhao Ziyang.* New York: Simon and Schuster, 2009.

Zheng, Yongnian. *Discovering Chinese Nationalism in China: Modernization, Identity, and International Relations.* New York: Cambridge University Press, 1999.

Zweig, David. *Internationalizing China: Domestic Interest and Global Linkages.* Ithaca, NY: Cornell University Press, 2002.

Index

About the Author

Guoli Liu is a professor of political science at the College of Charleston. His main teaching and research interests are comparative politics and international relations, with an emphasis on East Asia. He is the author of *States and Markets: Comparing Japan and Russia* (Westview Press, 1994) and, with Deng Peng and Xiaobing Li, *United States Foreign Policy and Sino-American Relations* [in Chinese] (China Social Sciences Press, 2000). His edited books include *Chinese Foreign Policy in Transition* (Aldine Transaction, 2004); with Lowell Dittmer, *China's Deep Reform: Domestic Politics in Transition* (Rowman and Littlefield, 2006); and, with Quansheng Zhao, *Managing the China Challenge: Global Perspectives* (Routledge, 2009).

www.ingramcontent.com/pod-product-compliance
Lightning Source LLC
Chambersburg PA
CBHW072001260326
41914CB00004B/883